TAKING THE SHORT TACK (SECOND EDITION)

CREATING INCOME AND CONNECTING WITH READERS

MATTY DALRYMPLE

MARK LESLIE LEFEBVRE

WILLIAM KINGSFIELD PUBLISHERS

Matty dedicates this book to her friends at Table 25— Michael Bradley, Jane Gorman, Jane Kelly, James McCrone, Lisa Regan, and Diane Vallere—for their steadfast support, and to her husband, Wade Walton, for being her most faithful beta reader.

Mark dedicates this book to Kristine Kathryn Rusch and Dean Wesley Smith, for the constant reminder of the power of short fiction and the inspiration to continue to learn and to experiment within publishing. And to Douglas Smith, who suggested that Mark needed to get himself to Kris and Dean's fantastic workshops.

PART 1
STARTING THE VOYAGE

INTRODUCTION

Are you a short fiction writer wondering what opportunities that work opens?

Are you a long-form fiction writer wondering if short fiction is worth the investment of your time?

This book will provide the answers—and the time is right.

The appetite for short story collections is still strong, with new bestselling collections from both established and emerging authors: *The Women* by Kristin Hannah (Goodreads Choice Award winner), *Green Frog* by Gina Chung (National Book Award nominee), and *Upright Women Wanted* by Sarah Gailey. ("The best short story books and collections for 2025" https://www.panmacmillan.com/blogs/literary/best-short-stories-short-story-collections) Short stories that tackle issues around gender, race, and social justice especially resonate with audiences, and publishers seek out collections covering these themes. ("Market Analysis of Short Story Books in 2025" https://www.accio.com/business/best_selling_short_story_books)

Short fiction is uniquely suited to our increasingly fast-paced lives and decreasingly available free time. Readers are looking for stories they can consume during their train ride to work, while waiting to pick up the kids from soccer practice, over their lunch break—even over their coffee break.

And as Geoff Shaw says in his online course "How to Succeed with Kindle Short Reads," sometimes the reader doesn't want the feast of an entire novel. Sometimes they just want a snack of short fiction. Or perhaps they really do want a feast, but they are more likely to go to *your* feast—to read *your* novels—if they have a little *amuse-bouche* of a piece of your short fiction to whet their appetite.

Or, to apply the nautical metaphor that Matty uses for the writing craft and the publishing voyage, sometimes what you want is a trip on an ocean liner, but sometimes what you want is a jaunt in an elegantly crafted dory.

Despite the technical environment that has provided all the tools readers need to easily consume short fiction, as well as the societal environment that makes it an appealing option, the short fiction market is far less crowded than the novel market, at least in the independent publishing space. The writer who knows what's possible with short fiction can meet an under-served need.

We are enthusiastic about the opportunities short fiction offers the enterprising author for creating income and connecting with readers and offer this book to help you make the most of those opportunities.

Who Are We?

In 2015, Matty Dalrymple published the second Ann Kinnear Suspense Novel, *The Sense of Reckoning*—the follow-on to *The Sense of Death*—and planned to plunge into Book 3.

But another idea was clamoring for attention, and this idea became the first Lizzy Ballard Thriller, *Rock Paper Scissors*. Ann Kinnear fans wanted to know when Ann would be back, and Matty assured them that as soon as *Rock Paper Scissors* was launched, she'd return to Ann's adventures.

Rock Paper Scissors launched in 2017, to be followed by Lizzy Ballard Book 2: *Snakes and Ladders* in 2018 and Book 3: *The Iron Ring* in 2019.

The Ann Kinnear fans were not amused.

So, while working on the Lizzy Ballard books, Matty began writing Ann Kinnear Suspense Shorts to tide over the Ann fans.

As the stories began to collect, she had an idea for an ultimate goal: to assemble twelve stories, one set in each month of the year, to be published as a collection subtitled *A Year of Kinnear*.

But until those dozen stories were complete, what could be done with the individual stories as they were finished?

Retaining one as a reader magnet—a giveaway for subscribers to her e-mail newsletter—Matty published each on the major online retailers as a $0.99 (US) e-book, later raising the price to $1.99 to reflect shifting reader expectations and market conditions. She also contributed one to an anthology published to raise money for a local library and another to an anthology published by her Sisters in Crime chapter. But she believed there must be more that she could do with this work ... and she knew just the person to ask.

Matty followed Mark Leslie Lefebvre's *Stark Reflections on Writing and Publishing* podcast, and she sent Mark a request to devote an episode to sharing his knowledge on this topic.

Mark's own writing journey began with short fiction. His first short story appeared in print in 1992, the same year he started working in the book industry. At the time, the common wisdom for writers was to cut their chops selling short fiction to establish a name and a track record that would encourage an agent or editor to take them on for a full-length book. After a decade of selling short stories to various markets, and with digital publishing beginning to offer new opportunities for writers, Mark collected several of his previously published short fiction pieces and poetry into *One Hand Screaming*, a collection that he independently published in 2004.

Since then he has published novels and non-fiction books and has edited short fiction anthologies. But he has never lost his passion for short stories and continues to release them in a multitude of ways—including a return to that 2004 book. In the fall of 2024, Mark collected additional horror stories he had published and written in the two decades that followed the original release of his short story collection to produce a special revised and double-sized edition called *One Hand Screaming: 20 Haunting Years*.

The information Mark shared in his podcast about the opportunities for creating income and connecting with readers using short fiction led to an in-depth discussion between Matty and Mark that was too valuable to keep to ourselves. We agreed that an expanded version would be a great resource to other authors, novelists and short story scribes, traditionally published and independently published.

What is "Short Fiction"?

This book will follow the guidelines of the Science Fiction & Fantasy Writers Association to define short fiction:

Short story = up to 7,500 words

Novelette = 7,500-17,500 words

Novella = 17,500-40,000 words

SFWA considers anything over 40,000 words to be a novel.

Some other categories of short fiction include:

Drabble = exactly 100 words

<300 words = micro-fiction

<1,000 = flash fiction

This book will consider anything under 40,000 words to be short fiction.

Why "Short Tack"?

Anyone who has attended one of Matty's talks or read one of her articles on writing and publishing knows of her fondness for the nautical metaphor. It captures the idea that writing is a "craft" in both senses of the word, one that can be honed in a craftsman-like way, not one that requires the fickle muse to strike. The publishing experience is certainly a voyage, a trip that requires the person at the helm to adjust continuously for conditions, battening down for bad weather and capitalizing on the perfectly angled wind when it comes. And we as authors owe it to our readers to send them off on their journey in a well-built, seaworthy vessel.

The nautical metaphor continues to work for the topic of this book: how to make the most of our short fiction.

Wikipedia defines "short tack" as "to tack several times in rapid succession when sailing upwind in a narrow waterway." We'll see in this book how the rapid release of short fiction can help you make the most of opportunities posed by the always-changing winds of the marketplace.

A national champion sailing instructor says, "From a racing perspective it is generally faster to make several short tacks over a distance of a racecourse. Here is why: while moving up the racecourse a sailor has the opportunity to read and react to shifts. There are ALWAYS wind shifts, no matter how small." Replace "wind" with "market" in that last sentence, and you'll get a preview of how authors can use short fiction to test the waters of new opportunities—"several short tacks"—rather than with one larger work.

The website Skipper Tips advises, "If your engine dies one

day—and you can bet it will—the ability to 'short-tack' could be vital to know." We'll discuss how you can use short fiction to get unstuck in a longer work.

And Sailing World recommends the short tack when "you're sailing toward more wind, getting a better lane, or sailing towards a significant gain, such as favorable current." We will definitely be exploring how you can take advantage of today's favorable currents for short fiction.

So what are those currents?

Read on.

Why Short Fiction … and Why Now?

Through the first half of the twentieth century, there was a significant market for short fiction—*Colliers, Cosmopolitan, Esquire*—and significant names writing for it—Hemingway, Fitzgerald, Asimov, Chandler. In fact, Matty's father, Thomas William Dalrymple, writing under the pen name William Kingsfield (which became the name of Matty's indie imprint) had short stories published in all three of those magazines. Kristine Kathryn Rusch estimates that there were 12,000 slots available per year in the traditional short fiction publishing market. However, by the end of the 1950s, this market had collapsed, and the remaining short fiction players were largely focused on genre fiction (science fiction, fantasy, mystery, thriller, and, to a lesser extent, romance).

There followed a period where short fiction authors had only a small, genre-limited, and highly competitive market to which to pitch their works.

Then the digital revolution arrived, and two changes led to a surge of new opportunities.

One was the lower cost to short fiction publishers to set up a digital platform than a print platform. As Jason Sanford says in

"The State of the Genre Magazine," "the boon of e-publishing has lowered the traditional printing and distribution cost barriers to creating new genre magazines. This allows more people than ever, including marginalized and diverse voices, to create their own magazines without the need for a large company or trust fund to support their dreams."

The second change that paved the way for short fiction opportunities was the easy access to content that e-readers provided. Readers were just a few taps away from a story that was exactly what they were looking for at that moment.

These changes provided easier publication of, and access to, all content, but the opportunities for short fiction in particular increased due to another development: our increasingly fast-paced lifestyles. People who might not be able to invest the time to read a full novel can grab time over lunch or during their commute (audio only if you're behind the wheel!) to enjoy a piece of short fiction.

Platforms that market specifically to this niche have come and gone over the years. Wattpad has been a mainstay platform for short fiction, and for every Kindle Vella and Yonder and Radish that shuts down, other platforms rise to take their place: Laterpress, SerialTeller, Dreame, Inkitt, Tapas. These platforms make short fiction works instantly accessible to time-strapped readers.

Easy access to a plethora of great short fiction that fits well into busy schedules is the benefit for the reader. But what are the benefits to the writer of short fiction?

How Do You Benefit?

For the writer, *short* means faster to produce. Writers may be able to produce an eight-thousand-word short story in a tenth of the time that they produce an eighty-thousand-word novel. In fact, they may be able to produce it even more quickly than that because short fiction doesn't include the plotting complexities that can be such a time-consuming part of creating a novel-length work.

The speed of production enables you to dip your toe in a new genre or world or set of characters before investing the time to jump into a full-length novel. It also gives you the opportunity to present new material to current and potential fans much more frequently than you could with novel-length works, upping short fiction's value as a reader connection tool.

Faster creation means that whatever goal you have for your short fiction—income creation or reader connection—you will have many more pieces of work with which to pursue that goal.

If you are seeking to make money from your short fiction by publishing it as a standalone e-book, then having ten eight-thousand-word short stories available for $1.99 each may well earn you more money than having one eighty-thousand-word novel available for $6.99.

However, we want to add an important caveat.

The greater output of short fiction must be based on its shorter length and decreased complexity in comparison to novel-length work, NOT on lower quality.

Whether selling your short fiction or giving it away as a marketing tool, the work must tell a compelling story in a polished style appropriate to the genre and be free of grammatical or typographical errors. If you want people to read your creative work, you owe it to them to give them the best possible experience, regardless of the length of the work.

The Goals

Authors interested in learning more about the opportunities offered by short fiction are usually interested in two different—

although not mutually exclusive—goals: **creating income** from their short fiction and using it as a tool to **connect with readers**.

Matty's initial interest was focused on connection—or, perhaps more specifically, reader relations. She wrote the first Ann Kinnear Suspense Short, *Close These Eyes*, as a way of tiding over her Ann fans while she worked on the Lizzy Ballard Thriller Trilogy. She only later became interested in exploring money-making opportunities based on this existing content.

Mark's love affair with short fiction began as a combination of working at continually refining his skills as a writer and working to build a pathway into traditional publishing. By the end of almost fifteen years of working the short fiction market and of refining his craft in the format, he realized he had a wealth of stories that could be repurposed. He had also learned that a short story was a unique storytelling medium that, unlike a novel, allowed him to explore and bring to fruition a concept in the limited bursts of time he had available to focus on writing.

We will examine opportunities for pursuing both income creation and reader connection goals using short fiction, and we will examine all current media—e-book, print, audio, video, even apps—within both the traditional and independent publishing markets.

WHAT YOU'LL FIND IN THIS BOOK

This book is divided into five sections:

1.Starting the Voyage provides an introduction to the topic of using short fiction for income creation and reader connection and provides definitions of the terms we will be using.

2.Creating Income covers money-making opportunities such as publication in traditional short fiction markets, e-books, and foreign language markets.

3.Connecting with Readers covers ways you can use short fiction to attract readers to your other works (e.g., the reader funnel) or to encourage them to engage with you (e.g., the reader magnet).

4.Best Practices covers strategies and tactics that apply across the income and reader connection goals. This section will make more sense after having read the details of the income or reader connection opportunities, so we've put it at the end, but ***don't skip this section!*** It will help you make the most of the ideas you choose to implement from the previous sections.

5.Resources Summary consolidates the "Resources" sections found at the end of each chapter.

DEFINITIONS

Below is a list of terms we will be using in this book.

Anthology – A grouping of works from different authors in a single book

Bundle – A grouping of works from the same or different authors in e-book format

Collection – A grouping of works from the same author in a single book

Reprints – Publication of a work that has been previously published

Rights / First and Second – *First rights* are the rights to a piece of work that has not been previously published; all subsequent sales are for *second rights* (there's no such thing as "third rights")

Short fiction – A work of less than 40,000 words, with the following subcategories:

Drabble = exactly 100 words

<300 words = micro-fiction

<1,000 = flash fiction

Short story = up to 7,500 words

Novelette = 7,500-17,500 words
Novella = 17,500-40,000 words

PART 2

CREATING INCOME

INTRODUCTION - CREATING INCOME

American crime writer and Mystery Writers of America Grand Master Lawrence Block has this to say about the income potential of short fiction in *The Liar's Companion: A Field Guide for Fiction Writers*:

While they may not be enormously lucrative, two days spent writing a short story puts more money in my pocket than two days of sitting and staring out the window. If I were to write, say, a story every other month, I'd be adding considerably to my overall body of work.

Besides, short stories pay off in surprising ways. They keep turning up in anthologies, bringing me a few dollars each time and keeping my name in front of readers. ... One story, written to keep a promise, won me an Edgar award and a Shamus award and, greatly expanded, became what is arguably my best novel. What kind of shortsightedness could lead me to the belief that short stories aren't worth writing?

To return to the nautical metaphor we introduced earlier, you can use the short tack—short fiction—for "sailing towards a significant gain, such as favorable current." We believe that the currents in the market have turned toward short fiction, and in this section, **Creating Income**, we will convince you, too, that short stories and other types of short fiction are well worth writing.

This section may be most applicable to writers who are primarily short fiction writers (versus the **Connecting with Readers** section, which may be more applicable to writers who are primarily novelists). However, it's worth reviewing both sections regardless of what you are currently writing because a concept that we categorize as related to connecting with readers may trigger ideas for income generation and vice versa.

The Science Fiction & Fantasy Writers Association (SFWA) defines pro rates for short fiction as $0.08 (US) per word, so it is true that no matter how prolific you are, and no matter how many of your stories are accepted for publication, it's difficult to get rich on short fiction alone. However, it can be a meaningful income stream to supplement earnings from other work.

The retail and publishing industries are always shifting and evolving, and writers can't rely on things always working the way they have in the past. Income streams that are profitable today might disappear tomorrow. Change is the only constant.

Business-savvy authors have learned that diversifying their income streams is key. And diversity isn't just about publishing your work to multiple retail and library platforms; it's about experimenting with different formats and media as well.

The digital revolution taught us that a book doesn't need to be three-hundred pages bound between two pieces of cloth. It can be whatever works for end consumers to satisfy their desire for content on any platform and in any medium.

Therefore, experimentation in format, in form, in style, and in length is vital, as is experimenting to find different ways that a single piece of short fiction can find new life via the multiple formats now available for authors to exploit.

The profitability of short fiction relies not only on producing great work, making the effort to find a home for it, and a bit of luck, but also on the mindset that every piece of short fiction you write offers many opportunities for income creation and reader connection—create once, publish and promote everywhere. In fact, Lawrence Block in the quote referenced above is practicing this principle, since *The Liar's Companion* is a compilation of columns he wrote for *Writer's Digest* magazine.

It's not necessary for you to pick just one of the ideas in this section for each of your short stories: you can potentially benefit from many of these approaches for a single piece of short fiction ***assuming that you have retained the legal rights to do so***. (More on that in the chapter on "Rights Licensing" in the **Best Practices** section.)

In this section on **Creating Income**, we will cover:

- **Traditional Publishing Market** – The most well-established way of creating income from your short fiction
- **Third-party Anthologies** – Among the most powerful tools that a short fiction author has to pursue both income and reader connection goals
- **Self-Published Anthologies and Collections** – How self-publishing tools and platforms enable authors to pursue these opportunities for themselves
- **Standalone e-books** – Guidelines for applying the same tools and platforms available in the

independent publishing world for long-form fiction to short fiction

- **Collections** – An examination of the benefits of publishing a grouping of your own works
- **Libraries** – An overview of this often-overlooked outlet for reaching readers
- **Serials and Subscriptions** – An exploration of the ways short fiction authors can benefit from the increasing popularity of serial stories
- **Contests** – Opportunities to gain recognition and sometimes earn income through prize money or anthology inclusion
- **Audio** – A vital platform for short fiction as well as longer works
- **Patron Support** – Services that enable committed fans to provide financial support
- **Foreign Language Markets** – A sometimes overlooked opportunity to reach a global audience
- **Getting Unstuck** – Benefits of using short fiction as a way to step back from a work whose engine has died

TRADITIONAL PUBLISHING MARKET

Selling your story to a publication via the traditional publishing market is the most well-established way of creating income from your short fiction. This approach has several advantages:

- It can provide up-front income: someone is paying you for the privilege of publishing your work. Payment for short stories usually comes comparatively quickly and is not spread out over years based on milestones such as *contract signing*, *delivery of manuscript*, and *publication date*, as is often the case for book-length works.
- You work with an editor who can not only help you polish your piece of short fiction but also enable further connections within this world.
- Once you've found a home for your short fiction work, and after you have made the requested edits, your work is done; the outlet that publishes your work handles any design elements and the production and distribution of the work.

- Having your work published via a traditional publishing market, especially a prestigious one, carries a cachet you don't always get with independently published works.

NOTE: *A vital part of tapping into traditional publishing platforms to get your short stories into the hands of readers is to have a firm understanding of the implications of granting rights to your intellectual property to third parties; carefully review the chapter on "Rights Licensing" in the **Best Practices** section before pursuing these opportunities.*

Researching Markets

There are numerous resources available to help you find possible markets for your short fiction work.

The *Writer's Market*'s annual guide is one of the best-known and most long-established resources and covers every genre of short fiction. Online resources include Duotrope and Submittable.

In these resources, you'll find thousands of options for your short fiction, so it's important to prioritize your outreach. Prioritization is important for two reasons. First, submissions take time, and you want to invest that time wisely. Second, since prestigious publications are less likely to publish reprints—works that have previously been published elsewhere—you don't want to reduce your chances of an acceptance by one of these platforms by having a work published first in a less desirable publication. Start at the top of your "most wanted" list and work your way down.

Prioritizing Options

Prestige

Acceptance of a story by a more prestigious and well-known magazine or anthology is a signal to the literary community of the story's merit. These publications are often also automatically included in submissions for major literary prizes such as the Pushcart Prize or the O. Henry Award, or for inclusion in annual collections like *Best American Short Stories.*

These larger and more well-established markets often have a larger audience reach which can lead to more visibility for an author's brand. They are also more likely to be considered for review by critics and discovered by booksellers and librarians. If an author's goal is to attract a literary agent, having stories published in high profile and esteemed short story markets can be valuable, since editors and agents often keep an eye on these markets for discovering emerging talent.

Finally, the more prestigious markets tend to offer a far more generous payment for accepted stories, far surpassing the industry standard terms of $0.08 per word as the minimum pro rate for short fiction.

Rates

As of this writing, the Science Fiction & Fantasy Writers Association (SFWA) quotes $0.08 (US) per word as a pro rate. Rates decrease from there through semi-pro and token (e.g., copies of the publication in which the story appears).

As you assess the markets to which you will submit your work, consider your goals. When Mark first started his writing journey, he was happy to receive a token payment—for example, a contributor's copy of the magazine—for his work. Once he had refined his writing skills and built his name, his goal shifted to income creation, and his strategy changed to submitting to markets paying semi-pro or pro rates. However, there's no reason not to start at the higher-paying end of the spectrum and work your way toward lower-paying platforms as needed, especially if you follow our advice for refining your work as described in the section on "Behind the Curtain: Insights from the Curator's Desk" in the **Best Practices** section. A decision to submit to a publication offering only token payments may make sense, especially early in your short fiction career. In fact, there will be circumstances in which you might want to grant the right for a platform to publish your work for no compensation—for example, to support a charity or cause. But in general, a reputable publishing market should not ask you to pay them to publish your story.

Availability of Publication

If the publication is one that is available in print, consider how widely it will be distributed. Will you be able to go to your favorite local bookstore and see it on the shelf or magazine rack? Is it a publication that is carried by library systems? Sometimes the publication's website will indicate where it will be available. Sometimes you can determine the breadth of distribution via the *Writer's Market* write-up. If necessary, consult with your local bookstore or library.

Literary Citizenship Opportunities

As we mention in the discussion of **Rates** above, some special projects and anthologies are created to raise funds for a charity or special cause, with authors donating their work to the project without compensation.

For example, Mark has offered original stories and reprints to nearly half a dozen anthology projects to benefit causes he wants to support. One of those projects is a charity anthology that Superstars Writing Seminars creates to raise funds for endowments and scholarships to the annual conference that teaches the business of writing and publishing. Matty has donated stories without compensation to an anthology celebrating the thirtieth anniversary of her chapter of Sisters in Crime and to another anthology supporting a local public library. As advocates for writers, Mark and Matty are happy to waive professional rates in order to support these causes.

That is not to say that there are no benefits for the authors in these circumstances. The Superstars anthologies Mark has contributed to are curated by respected editor Lisa Mangum and are often reviewed by science fiction and fantasy trade journals. There is also a special in-person event related to the annual anthology's launch which can offer further networking opportunities for contributors.

Submission Process

For strategic considerations related to making short fiction submissions, see the chapter "Behind the Curtain: Insights from the Curator's Desk" in the **Best Practices** section. Below we outline some of the more tactical considerations related to the submission process.

Submission Mechanism

You should consider the relative ease or difficulty of the submission process itself, since an hour spent on a submission is an hour you are not spending on something else, such as writing. On one hand, you could choose to streamline the submission process as much as possible by eliminating any platforms that require a postal submission. (Almost all platforms accept electronic submissions.) On the other hand, it is possible that the markets that receive postal submissions might be less inundated with a large number of submissions and might be easier to break into. Either approach makes sense—just consider the pros and cons of each for your own situation.

Simultaneous Submission

If a particular market or publication indicates that it accepts simultaneous submissions, you can send that same piece of short fiction to other publications at the same time as long as those markets also accept simultaneous submissions. You run the "risk" of having multiple markets ask to publish your story and you'll have to accept just one of those offers, but if you're going to have a dilemma in your navigation of the traditional publishing game, this is the one to have!

Reprints

Print and online market information resources will enable you to find markets that accept reprints—short fiction that has previously been published elsewhere. Note that if you have published a piece of short fiction on any platform, *even if you have received no royalties for it* (for example, publishing the story in your author newsletter or on your blog, or contributing a story to an anthology raising money for a charitable cause), then you must submit that story as a reprint.

Rates for reprints are usually lower than for first rights works. However, if you've played your contractual cards right and retained the second rights to a work (i.e., any publication rights after its first publication), any income you get for reprints is found money (or, as a sailor might say, *money for old rope*).

Submission Tracking

Effective tracking of your short story submissions is key to ensure both that you comply with the requirements for each market and that you are making the most of the income generation and reader connection opportunities of each work. To track your short story submissions, create two spreadsheets, one for the stories and one for the markets, including the fields listed below, as well as any other data you feel would be helpful for your own situation.

For each **story**, capture the following information:

- Metadata - Story title / Word count / Genre / Themes (e.g., noir, Christmas, vampires)
- Repeat data for each submission - Market submitted to / Submission date / Response / Response date
- If accepted - Agreement date / Publication date (if appropriate) / Terms (e.g., not submittable to other publications for reprint for one year from X date) / Payment amount / Payment status (Pending, Received ... might include contributor copies of publication)

For each **market** to which you submit a story, capture the following information:

- Name of Market (e.g., *Lamplight, Ellery Queen Mystery Magazine*)
- Reprints accepted?
- Submission site URL
- Format standard (e.g., William Shun's short story format)
- Typical response time

You can find an Excel spreadsheet that you can use to capture this information at theindyauthor.com/short-tack.

The Waiting Game

As you will see as you begin your research, different publications and markets give different timeframes within which you can expect a response. Be sure to note these times in your tracking document—if you are pursuing publication in the traditional short fiction market, then you can't avoid playing the waiting game. A record of the expected response time will enable you to set your expectations appropriately.

Of course, all publications will let you know if they are

interested in your story, and most publications will let you know if they are not. However, there are always those for whom "no response means *no*" (even if their guidelines state otherwise).

In the same way that writing your next novel is a better way of increasing your sales than obsessively refreshing your sales dashboard, writing your next piece of short fiction and getting it started on its journey through the submission process is the best way to pave the way for success in this market.

Resources

Douglas Smith's *Playing the Short Game: How to Market and Sell Short Fiction* (2*nd* *Edition*)

The Indy Author Podcast Episode 193 - The Path to Short Story Publication with Michael Bracken

Submission Search Engines / Tools / Trackers

- Duotrope (duotrope.com) and Submittable (submittable.com) – Enable searches for appropriate markets; used by a number of traditional publishing platforms as their submission tool

Other Publication Listings

- *The Write Life* article "Where to Submit Short Stories: 23 Magazines and Websites That Want Your Work" (www.thewritelife.com/where-to-submit-short-stories/)

Submission Guidelines

- Proper Manuscript Format – Each market has its own submission guidelines (and violating them is a quick way into the reject pile) but William Shun's *Proper Manuscript Format* (www.shunn.net/format/story.html) is a reference cited by many markets. Note that one update to this venerable document is that submission in Courier font is no longer recommended.

THIRD-PARTY ANTHOLOGIES

We've divided our discussion of publications of **groupings** of short stories into two parts. We'll address the first scenario, where you are submitting your work to an editor / curator, in this chapter, "Third-party Anthologies." We'll address the second scenario, where you are acting as the editor / curator, in the next chapter, "Self-Published Anthologies and Collections."

Anthologies—groupings of works from different authors—are one of the most powerful tools that a short fiction author has to pursue both income and reader connection goals. The fact that the anthology includes many authors means that it can sell to the fan bases of all those authors, improving its potential for income generation. The fact that all those readers will be exposed not only to the work of their favorite author but also to the work of the other authors in the anthology means that the opportunity for connecting with new readers is high.

The component works in an anthology are often chosen based on specific genre (e.g., noir, horror, romance) and often on a specific theme (e.g., end-of-the-world, vampires, Christmas). They are often curated and edited by a recognized name. They can feature original works, include a mixture of new and reprint stories, or be themed reprint anthologies such as a *Year's Best Mystery Stories* collection.

They may be one-time projects—for example, *Noir at a Bar: The Oxford Files,* published by editor Gary Zenker to support the Oxford (PA) Public Library—or may be recurring—for example, *Tesseracts,* an annual science fiction and fantasy themed anthology that features Canadian writers. Mark served as editor for *Tesseracts Sixteen* and was a contributing author for *Tesseracts Seventeen.* A benefit of being published in a recurring anthology is that it has a proven track record and ongoing audience. Each year, bookstores and readers alike anticipate the next volume of that edition, providing a bit more visibility.

Inclusion in the most well-established and well-respected anthologies can come with impressive perks. For example, the annual *Writers of the Future* anthology—aimed at emerging writers who have not yet earned professional rates for short fiction or published a novel or novella—showcases their work to icons of the science fiction and fantasy field, including Larry Niven, Brandon Sanderson, Kevin J. Anderson, and Robert J. Sawyer. This anthology is widely available in bookstores around the world and comes with a significant marketing push from its publisher, Galaxy Press. In addition, participating authors have an opportunity to be mentored by the judges via an in-person week-long celebratory event in Los Angeles every spring that is connected to the launch of the book.

So how do you find these opportunities?

Finding the Opportunities

Writers improve their chances of success in anthology placements by being active members of their writing and publishing communities.

Unlike magazine and other serial short fiction markets,

anthologies tend to have short submission windows that are announced with limited lead times. In some cases, there is *no* call for submissions; instead, the editor requests stories from authors they are already familiar with or have previously worked with and whose work is appropriate for the anthology. Opportunities for inclusion in anthologies are often best found via word of mouth within writing groups and forums.

For example, for a horror-themed anthology that Mark edited in 2009, *Campus Chills*, he personally solicited stories from writers whose work he knew. While collecting stories for the anthology, Mark was on a panel with author James Alan Gardner at a science fiction conference. Mark knew James as a science fiction writer, but as they chatted while waiting for the panel to begin, Mark learned that Jim's first published story had been a horror tale. As a result of that informal discussion, Mark invited Jim to write a story for his anthology, for which the authors were paid professional rates.

Writers' groups are another great place to expand your contacts with fellow authors. Matty was invited to participate in the anthology *Noir at a Bar: The Oxford Files* through a writers' group connection with its editor, Gary Zenker. Hanging out and sharing ghostly tales in the hotel lobby late one night at Superstars Writing Seminars was the genesis of the brainstorm that led to the anthology *Cursed Collectibles* which Mark was invited to submit to.

In another example of how developing personal relationships within the industry creates opportunities, Kevin J. Anderson invited Mark to submit a story to an anthology while enjoying poutine and craft beer on a patio in Hamilton, Ontario. The anthology contained stories based on songs from the Canadian rock band Rush called *2113: Stories Inspired by the Music of Rush*, and Kevin knew Mark shared his appreciation of the band.

Must you cultivate an interest in French Canadian cuisine and craft beer to take advantage of the opportunities presented by anthologies? No ... but you do improve your likelihood of being invited to participate in an anthology by being a good citizen of the writing community. If you've supported a fellow author, they're more likely to think of you if they are curating an anthology, or if they know someone who is. Reference the chapter "Being an Active Member of the Community" in the **Best Practices** section for more on this.

When new opportunities come your way, how do you decide if they're worth pursuing? Below are a few things to keep in mind.

Assessing Prestige

Who are the other contributors, and who will be penning the introduction? This information might not be available at the time of submission, but if the anthology is recurring, you can get a sense of the caliber of the participating authors by reviewing previous installments. Prestigious anthologies will often include a well-known author to draw people to it: Nora Roberts for romance, Stephen King for horror, Michael Connelly for police procedurals. These marquee names will attract fans who will buy the anthology because of that person's recommendation or contribution but will end up discovering the other authors in the anthology.

Assessing Income Opportunity

How will participating authors be paid? For the more well-established anthologies, authors receive a **one-time upfront payment**, with amounts ranging from token payments through semi-pro rates and even up to pro rates. Payments can occur any

MATTY DALRYMPLE & MARK LESLIE LEFEBVRE

time between signing the contract to within 60 to 90 days of publication of the anthology. Authors do not receive any further payments regardless of how many units the anthology sells over the years.

For example, when Mark curated and published the anthology *Campus Chills* in 2009, he paid all thirteen contributors professional rates, which were, at the time, $0.05 USD per word. Mark paid roughly $3,700 for about 75,000 words across all the stories included in the anthology. As the publisher of this book, he kept all royalties for sales of the book, which is still available. (As of the end of 2024, the anthology had brought in close to $5,200 USD in sales.)

Other anthologies offer no up-front payment but **share royalties** with participating authors. Payment splitting is far more common within the indie author community than with traditional outlets. This is where authors do not receive any payment in advance but instead receive a percentage of the royalties from those sales. The main benefit of an anthology like this for the editor is that they do not have to raise the funds to pay for the stories upfront. The potential benefit to the authors included in the anthology is they can continue to earn revenue for years after a book is released.

As examples, let's take a look at two of the anthologies Mark was paid up front for. Mark received $0.05 USD per word for his stories in 2113 and *Northern Haunts*. *Northern Haunts* was released in 2008 and Mark earned $100 for this reprint story. 2113 was published in 2016 and Mark earned $265 for this original story. Both books are still available for sale online and in bookstores. Extrapolating sales based on BookScan weekly sales reports and ongoing tracking and analysis of Amazon ranking for both titles, it is very unlikely that Mark would have earned even $100 from ongoing royalties in the more than 17 years since *Northern Haunts* was first released. (It contains 100 stories, and his share of earnings would likely be no more than 1%).

However, with the 18 contributors for 2113 and a split per contributor of about 5%, it's entirely possible Mark would have earned considerably more via a royalty split than via the upfront payment. Since its release nearly ten years ago, 2113 has been a consistent seller, with global fans of the rock band Rush continuing to discover it. While the book's exact sales are known only by the publisher, Mark estimates that it has sold tens of thousands of copies over the years. Assuming that 50,000 copies have sold and that revenue from those sales might amount to $3.50 per unit (based on industry averages on margin earned on a print book), a 5% royalty share (that is, 5% of the earned margin) would be upwards of $8,750.

Of course, these examples of *Northern Haunts* and 2113 are complete speculation, because they were traditionally published titles that didn't have payment splitting as an option.

A third, less common, option for paying contributors is for the publisher to offer **both a token upfront payment and a royalty share**. The upfront pay offered is usually less than pro or even semi-pro rates and might often be a flat fee. This option allows the curator to offer a bit of monetary incentive to the participating authors as well as the opportunity to earn even more should the anthology be successful and sell numerous copies.

One example is the 2020 anthology *Obsessions* that Mark published. Because he raised the funds to pay professional rates to the anthology contributors through a Kickstarter campaign, he not only paid the 15 collaborators professional rates for their fiction (which came to about $4,000 USD), but he also leveraged Draft2Digital's payment splitting option for the print and e-book sales with a 5% royalty on sales. In the five years that the book has been out, each contributor has earned an additional $35 dollars.

That might not seem like a lot of money, but for authors who leverage multiple channels for the same short story, they might have also sold reprint rights to that same piece of work, and thus the additional $35 in royalties is yet another drop that slowly fills their bucket.

Not every legitimate indie anthology will be a direct income earner; you can also gain goodwill and the possibility of reader connections leading to sales by **donating a piece of short fiction** to an anthology to support a good cause. Matty donated her Ann Kinnear Suspense Short "Our Dancing Days" to *Noir at a Bar: The Oxford Files* to support the Oxford (PA) Public Library. She contributed her short story "All Deaths Endure" and a story coauthored with fellow crime fiction author Jane Gorman, "Blood of the Wicked," to an anthology assembled by the Delaware Valley Sisters in Crime of short stories set in and around Philadelphia: *Death Knell VI*. Mark donated a reprint of his story "Requiem" to the anthology *Cursed Collectibles*, which supported the Don Hodge Memorial Scholarship to Superstars Writing Seminars, an annual Colorado Springs conference at which Mark is a regular instructor.

Note that publishing a story in such an anthology, even if you're not making any money from it, still counts as publication, and so you would have to submit such a story to other markets as a reprint, not as a first rights work.

Assessing Production

How will the anthology be produced? Anthologies that will be offered in print are the most desirable. As Jason Sanford says in "The State of Genre Magazines," "Just as e-books have not come close to replacing print books over the last decade despite many predictions this would happen, so have print editions of genre magazines held on in the marketplace. As Sheila Williams of *Asimov*'s told me, part of this is due to many readers still preferring print editions. But she also added, 'Print editions are much more visible. They do a lot of our promotion for us.'"

Anthologies for which the publisher will produce stock in print runs (as opposed to a print-on-demand / POD publication where the books are only manufactured upon order by a bookstore or consumer) will be far more likely to be stocked by bookstores, often displayed at the beginning of its genre's section.

Another option to pursue to make your story available to anthology curators is to upload it to an online marketplace designed for this purpose, such as **PubShare** (formerly BundleRabbit). Independent curators (not PubShare itself) select stories from the marketplace for digital anthologies or bundles. Curators can identify a set of books that conform to a certain theme, as reflected in the story's metadata, then request you as the author to approve your book to be included in that bundle. Curators can make these bundles available for extended periods, and the longer the anthology is available, the longer it will continue to earn you and your anthology partners money.

The benefit of a platform like PubShare is that it handles some of the tedious administrative work required of other outlets. As a potential contributor, once your story is loaded to PubShare, your work is (theoretically) done. We say *theoretically* because, as with participation in any anthology, you will greatly increase your chances of inclusion through some author-to-author marketing and networking with the platform's curators.

For the curator, PubShare handles the compiling of individual stories into a single anthology or collection and then making it into a single epub file.

Your Responsibility as a Participating Author

Prestige, income, and the chance to see your story in an anthology on bookstore shelves are all benefits the editor of an anthology might bring to you as a contributing author. What do you owe the editor if your story is chosen for inclusion in the anthology?

You have a responsibility to promote the anthology to your fans and followers in your e-mail newsletter, on social media, and on any other platform you use to connect with your readers. Make sure your curator knows about your marketing efforts—for example, ask permission to add them to your e-mail newsletter distribution list or flag them in your social media posts. If your curator knows that you are doing your bit to spread the word about the anthology, you increase the chance that they will choose your work for a future anthology.

But you're not just doing this for the publisher or anthology editor. Every time you push or promote the book, you're helping to raise the visibility of every other author in that anthology. You never know where or when that community-minded elevation of the group of participating authors will help you in the long run. And, of course, continue to elevate your own brand by spotlighting any anthology that contains one of your stories.

Red Flags to Watch Out For

While most traditional anthology editors are genuinely committed to serving both their readers and their participating authors, every venture carries the risk of encountering bad players whose practices can undermine your work and reputation. Some anthologies operate less as genuine publishing opportunities and more as revenue streams for the organizer. As you assess anthology calls, keep an eye out for these warning signs:

- **Every submission is included** – Be wary of anthologies that promise publication to every entrant. This practice dilutes the value of your inclusion and often indicates a pay-to-play model rather than true editorial selection.
- **No real editing** – A strong anthology benefits from an engaged editor shaping the anthology. If there's no sign of meaningful editorial involvement, you may be looking at a vanity project rather than a professional opportunity.
- **Mandatory book purchases** – If acceptance requires you to buy a minimum number of copies of the anthology, think twice. Legitimate anthologies may offer contributor discounts, but they shouldn't make purchases a condition of inclusion.
- **Inflated prices, minimal distribution** – Some anthologies are priced far higher than market norms and have no realistic distribution strategy. Readers outside the contributors' circle rarely encounter them, limiting income and visibility. This is another sign that the people producing the anthology make their money when participating authors purchase copies rather than by selling to the open market.
- **Misleading claims of prestige** – Some projects use vague or deceptive language to suggest associations with respected organizations, awards, or well-known authors. Verify any claims before committing.

- **Rights grabs and no royalties** – Always read the contract. Beware of anthologies that demand broad or perpetual rights, especially without royalties or clear compensation. Any license you grant should be limited in scope and time.
- **Royalty fraud** – In revenue-sharing anthologies, insist on transparent reporting and clear royalty-splitting mechanisms. Lack of clarity around how and when royalties will be distributed is a major red flag.

SELF-PUBLISHED ANTHOLOGIES

We've divided our discussion of publications of **groupings** of short stories into two parts. In the chapter "Third-party Anthologies," we addressed the scenario where you are submitting your work to an editor / curator for consideration. In this chapter, we'll address the scenario where you are acting as the editor / curator.

What if, despite your active engagement in your writing and publishing communities, you aren't finding opportunities for placement of your stories in anthologies?

For ultimate control over the anthology, consider acting as the editor / curator. In this role, you choose what work is included and from which authors, manage the cover design, and create marketing copy. You are responsible for communicating on an ongoing basis with the participating authors, providing them with the materials with which to promote the anthology (for example, images or text to use on social media or their websites), incenting them to actively promote the work, handling administrative tasks like distributing royalties (if royalties are to be distributed), and more.

The role of editor / curator also comes with the opportunity for increased income since the anthology curator generally gets a bigger share of the royalties than the participating authors to compensate them for this extra work.

Before deciding to take on this role, consider the time it will take (and, as always, weigh the benefits against other uses to which you might put this time, like writing). The time investment will be not just in the reading, editing, and publishing work, but in all of the additional tasks that come with overseeing an entirely new publication. Remember that unlike publishing an indie book that is solely your own work, you'll be juggling a host of complex unknowns involving many other people, each with their own creative vision.

The Role of the Editor / Curator

Should you choose to take on this role, here are some curatorial tips:

- **Determine the goal** – Anthologies are both an income creation strategy and a reader connection opportunity; consider which of these is primary because it will impact other decisions you make about your anthology (as described below).
- **Determine the number of participating authors** – The more authors who are represented in an anthology, the more cross-promotional opportunities there are, and the more sales opportunities there will be due to the large number of interested readers that the participating authors bring. However, a large number of authors also means that the proceeds will be split across a large number of people. Match the number of contributors to the goals of the anthology.

- **Determine the authors to approach** – You may be tempted to stick to the safe path of inviting authors you know personally to participate in the anthology. However, unless at least one of those authors has an established following, you are limiting your income creation and reader connection opportunities. Consider approaching authors who are a bit ahead of you in their author careers, and consider giving them added incentive to participate, such as a higher percentage of the royalties. As always, weigh the potential benefit of enlisting a particular author to your anthology against the time needed to pursue those authors and the likelihood of them accepting your invitation. You could invest a couple of hours crafting an invitation to Stephen King to participate in your horror anthology (with, we predict, little chance of success) or spend those couple of hours approaching an established but not-currently-bestselling author (with a greater chance of success).

- **Communicate Goals and Expectations** – Clearly share your goals for the anthology with prospective contributors so they can evaluate whether their own objectives align. Transparency helps ensure everyone is committed to the plan required to achieve those goals. For example, if your aim is to generate steady income over time, participating authors must be willing to keep their stories in the anthology for an extended period.

Managing the Process

The same independent publishing technologies that have empowered authors to get their novels in front of readers without navigating the gauntlet of traditional publishing gate-keepers are available for short fiction as well, and they put participating in and even curating short fiction anthologies within reach of any enterprising author. Tools like Scrivener and Vellum greatly ease the process of taking multiple individual files and combining them into one file for your anthology.

There are also services such as Draft2Digital that handle the division of royalties from sale of the anthologies across the curator and the participating authors. They can accommodate variations across royalties, such as providing the curator with a higher percentage of the royalties to help compensate them for the work needed to curate the anthology or providing a well-known writer with a higher percentage to encourage them to participate in the anthology. Online marketplaces like PubShare, described in the chapter "Third-party Anthologies," are another nicely automated option.

Think carefully before using platforms that will require you to distribute royalties manually. Sending a cut of the royalties to a dozen anthology participants might seem manageable at first, but remember that you will need to be handling this tedious administrative task for years or even decades after the publication of the work. In addition, consider the challenges of paying authors from different countries. Mark lives in Canada and has collaborated with authors from the USA and the UK. Having to convert payments from book sales into Canadian dollars and then re-converting those funds to USD and GBP usually results in conversion rate losses—not to mention the additional time spent performing these calculations and the costs involved in the transfer of money between countries.

Online Reading Lists

You can create a virtual anthology or collection via an online grouping of themed works such as that enabled by the free Books2Read Reading Lists service. This tool allows you to assemble a curated list of links to separate published books and short stories into a single, shareable page. Each link within Books2Read is a Universal Book Link, directing readers to their preferred retailer (e.g., Amazon, Apple Books, Barnes & Noble, Kobo). You can customize the list title, description, and order of the works within each carousel and even include genre or theme tags to help readers navigate.

This is an excellent option if you want to promote a group of stories without doing the additional work to combine them into a single e-book file. For example, you might create a seasonal horror story collection, a sampler from your backlist, or a show-case of work from members of your writing group.

We created an example of one such page, "Tales from the Shadows," that contains a carousel of Matty's Ann Kinnear Suspense Shorts and a collection of a number of standalone short story e-books from Mark. Check it out at https://book s2read.com/rl/shadowtales

Once your list is created, you can share the URL in newsletters, social media, or print materials using QR codes. (Reference the chapter "Links and QR Codes" in the Best Practices section for more on creating and distributing such links effectively.)

COLLECTIONS

Independent publishing offers another opportunity that is not common in the traditional publishing market: the ability to create a collection (i.e., a grouping of works from one author) for an author whose name is not part of the literary canon (at least not yet).

Mark's very first published book, which appeared in 2004 was a self-published collection of short stories and poems that he called *One Hand Screaming*. The volume comprised mostly reprints of horror stories that had previously appeared in small press magazines and some anthologies.

But you don't need to have a full-length book to put something like this together. Mark has also created numerous mini story collections of tales that originally sold to small press print horror magazines. Leveraging the reprint rights on these stories, he repackaged them into themed collections that run anywhere from 8000 to 16,000 words in length. He calls them "digital chapbooks."

Some examples of these mini story collections:

- *Snowman Shivers* – Two dark humor stories featuring snow men
- *Bumps in the Night* – Four short stories meant to be read around the campfire
- *Active Reader* – Three "Twilight Zone" style tales about the book world
- *Z is for Zombie* – Three stories featuring zombies
- *Unexpected Strangers* – Three stories about encounters with strangers
- *Phantom Itch* – Four horror stories about ghosts, phantoms, and spirits

Once Matty has twelve Ann Kinnear Suspense Shorts, one for each month of the year, she plans to package them into a collection subtitled *A Year of Kinnear*.

Be sure to factor in the unique theme (in Mark's case) or universe / realm / characters (in Matty's case) when determining how and where to market these collected works. And remember that, in the same way you can leverage your reprint writes to sell stories to traditional markets, you can reuse them in your own collections. Mark's short story "Memento Mori" was published as a standalone story but also appears in his mini story collection *Ode to Classics*. His award-nominated tale "Erratic Cycles" not only appears in *One Hand Screaming* but was also used in the mini story collection *Bumps in the Night*.

When compiling stories for your book-length collection, consider leveraging two of your very best stories as the opening and closing tales in the book. Using a strong entry as the first story means that potential buyers browsing online will be able to see that story in the preview. And your closing story is the note that lingers—it's often what readers remember most once they've set the book down. Another strategy used by anthology editors is to put the third strongest story in the middle, creating a natural peak that keeps readers engaged through the center of the book and carries their interest to the end.

It's also important to consider that a well-crafted collection follows an overall narrative arc. For example the collection might feature similar styles or themed tales. In Mark's *One Hand Screaming: 20 Haunting Years*, he broke the collection into themed segments with their own original artwork and title. Those sections included flash fiction and poetry, Halloween stories, award-winning or award-nominated tales, and stories written with co-authors. Other times you might want to consider arranging stories based on the moods, the atmosphere, or even the genres. If you have a long, intense, and dark tale, for example, you might want to follow that up with a shorter, lighter, or even uplifting piece. This allows the reader some breathing space. It's not unlike the way you might consider the length of chapters in a novel, or perhaps even the length of sentences or paragraphs to control the pacing of the reading.

The process for publishing a collection of your own work has more in common with publishing a standalone e-book than with curating an anthology (a grouping of works from different authors) because you don't have to worry about aspects like obtaining or confirming rights from other authors or splitting royalties across multiple contributors. You can use a similar approach to that described in the chapter "Standalone e-books" to publish a collection of your short fiction in e-book format, and all the tools and technologies available for indie publishing print editions of a work are available to collections.

When pricing the collection, make sure it represents a discount from the sum of the costs of the individual stories, assuming they are also available à la carte, adding in a consideration of what the market will bear. You may need to experiment a bit to find out what readers of your genre are willing to pay for a collection. On Amazon, consider that any e-book priced over

$9.99 will mean a drop in royalties from 70% to 35%, and any print book priced under $9.99 will mean a drop in royalties from 60% to 50%.

You might also create a virtual collection, bringing together a selection of short fiction on a web page for easy reader access. In this scenario, you are giving up some control regarding how a reader will encounter and consume the content, but it is fast and easy to do using a free service like Books2Read Reading Lists and can be a great way to test out various combinations of content. Reference the chapter "Links and QR Codes" in the **Best Practices** section for more information.

STANDALONE E-BOOKS

In the previous chapters, we discussed income creation opportunities for short fiction in anthologies and collections, but you can publish your short fiction work in standalone format as well. All the same tools and platforms available in the independent publishing world for long-form fiction are applicable to short fiction as well. You can publish standalone e-books of a short story, novelette, or novella directly to retail platforms such as Amazon or Barnes & Noble or via distributors such as Draft2Digital. Publication of short fiction as standalone e-books is the route Matty chose for her Ann Kinnear Suspense Shorts.

The benefit of this approach for short fiction is the same as the benefit for any independently published work—what Matty likes to refer to as the Cs of indie publishing.

Creativity on Your Own Terms

Unlike traditional platforms, which often require a specific genre or theme, indie publishing your short fiction lets you follow your inspiration wherever it leads. For example, Matty can draw on any of professional spirit senser Ann Kinnear's consulting engagements as material for a short story. While these tales are popular with Ann's fans, they might be difficult to place in a traditional outlet.

Control

You have the ability to get your story into the hands of readers without navigating editorial gatekeepers and hoping to win one of the limited number of slots in their publications. (You also avoid the frustrations of working with sometimes-glitchy submission websites that stand between you and the traditional publishing editor.)

However, remember this counsel ...

Your ability to avoid third-party gatekeepers does not relieve you of the responsibility to produce a professional-grade product: a carefully crafted story that has been thoroughly edited and has an appealing and brand-right cover. *You must function as your own gatekeeper when assessing your work's readiness for publication.*

Chronology

You can plan for the chronology—the timing—of the release of your story, opening up marketing opportunities that are more difficult to coordinate if you're at the mercy of a third-party editor's publication schedule. You know that once you have your work edited and proofread to a professional standard and have a professional-grade cover ready, your short story can be available to your readers immediately.

The short time between completion of a piece of short fiction and being able to make it available to your readers allows you more easily to accommodate time-boxed opportunities related to holidays, anniversaries of historical events, even current news events. To reference the nautical metaphor we introduced earlier, Wikipedia defines "short tack" as "to tack several times in rapid succession when sailing upwind in a narrow waterway," and the rapid release of short fiction can help you make the most of opportunities posed by the always changing winds of the marketplace.

Cash – Minimal Outlay

The costs for producing these e-books can be low.

In the **Best Practices** section, we recommend how you can make some of the most expensive parts of professional indie publishing—professional-level editing and proofreading and professional-level cover design—affordable for these short works that will command lower prices.

ISBNs are another cost associated with indie publishing. As with any e-book, an ISBN is not required, and platforms offer either free identifiers (Amazon's ASIN), actual ISBNs (Draft2Digital), or dummy ISBNs (Kobo Writing Life). Draft2Digital's free ISBNs are *actual ISBNs* in that they are officially registered and recognized in the global book industry database, though Draft2Digital will appear as the publisher of record unless you provide your own. By contrast, Kobo Writing Life issues *dummy ISBNs* that function only within Kobo's system. These identifiers allow Kobo to process your e-book consistently, but they are not registered ISBNs and cannot be used outside the Kobo platform.

Owning your own ISBN and being listed as the publisher gives you full control over your book's metadata and reinforces your professional author brand. In the U.S., authors who plan to publish multiple standalone short stories as e-books can save money by purchasing a bundle of ISBNs through Bowker. For example, the per ISBN cost for a bundle of 10 ISBNs is about one-quarter the per ISBN cost when purchased individually, and if you anticipate publishing many short stories, the per ISBN savings is even greater with a bundle of 100 ISBNs, where each ISBN costs about one-twentieth what a single ISBN would cost.

In the current AI landscape, there's an emerging potential advantage of owning your own ISBN: an ISBN registered to you and showing you as the publisher of record can serve as a clear, verifiable data point linking you to a specific work. This could be useful in legal or administrative contexts—such as proving ownership when seeking compensation for use of your work in AI training datasets. That said, an ISBN is not a copyright registration and, by itself, may not constitute definitive proof of ownership. For full protection, U.S. authors should register their works with the U.S. Copyright Office.

In other English-language markets, the need to purchase ISBNs varies: Canadian and New Zealand authors can obtain them for free through their national libraries, while authors in the UK purchase them through the Nielsen ISBN Agency and authors in Australia purchase them through Thorpe-Bowker Identifier Services.

Cash – Small but Steady Income

Indie-published e-book short story standalones also offer the opportunity for small but steady income. As of mid-2025, Matty had earned almost $700 from her Ann Kinnear Suspense Shorts on various online retail platforms. Similarly, calculating just the online e-book sales of nine of his individually published short stories, Mark has earned a little over $1,000. We believe this is more than we would have earned had we sought placement in traditional outlets, especially when factoring in the time it takes to pursue such placements (and we should always assign a value to our time).

One of those platforms, Amazon, adds an interesting angle with their Kindle Short Reads. As with any book on Amazon, a customer can browse by genre, but with Kindle Short Reads, there's the extra dimension of time: Amazon categorizes the length of time they anticipate it will take to read the work in increments from fifteen minutes to two hours or more. This enables a genre fan with half an hour to kill on their train commute to find the perfect story to fill that available reading time.

However, even if readers know what they're looking for (e.g., a thirty-minute romance read), it takes some navigating to find these products. (We found that the easiest way to find them is not from the Amazon site but by Googling *kindle short reads*.) If a reader doesn't know that they're out there, they're unlikely to stumble across them.

But you can still use Amazon's categorization of short fiction by genre and anticipated reading time to increase sales. Even if a reader "in the wild" might have a hard time finding that thirty-minute romance story, you can still market to your followers using that extra information about anticipated reading time. You can also find short fiction comp authors by finding the top selling Short Reads authors within the genre and the duration of your story, and this is useful market research that can lead to increased sales.

Here are a few other Cs that authors should keep in mind for their indie-published short fiction.

Currency – Pricing Your Standalone Short Fiction

Unless you're a marquee-name author, you should keep the price of your short fiction e-books low; Matty prices hers at $1.99 (US), which feels like a fair counterpart to the $6.99 price of her full-length novels.

Some marketers might argue that since readers can often get full-length novels for $0.99, or even for free, they won't buy $1.99 short fiction. There are certainly readers out there whose first consideration when choosing their reading material is price, but these are not the readers you want to attract. You want to attract readers who love your genre, and those fans will be willing to make a modest investment for a great reading experience. In fact, you can have fun with the price in your marketing materials: "a brief interlude of romance for less than the cost of a single rose," "a short shot of suspense for a fraction of the cost of a double espresso."

You can take some of the sting out of offering your hard-won words at this low rate by knowing that, assuming you have retained the necessary rights, you can continue to earn income from this work through multiple uses of the same piece of work —for example, by including it in a higher-priced collection. Reference the chapter "Self-Published Anthologies and Collections" for more information.

Categories

The categories to which books are assigned on most retail platforms are adapted from the BISAC (Book Industry Standards and Communications) Subject Codes, which are managed and maintained by the BISG (Book Industry Study Group). Updated annually, there are over 3,500 BISAC Subject Codes and each retailer maps the official list to their own internal categories.

Indie authors who load their works to the online retail platforms can choose up to three different categories to which to assign a work, depending on the platform. BISG provides this advice of special interest to short fiction authors:

"FICTION / Anthologies (multiple authors)" and "FICTION / Short Stories (single author)" may be used with other subjects as appropriate: for example, a collection of ghost stories by several authors could be assigned "FICTION / Ghost" and "FICTION / Anthologies (multiple authors)" (it is recommended that the subject describing the genre be assigned first). Note that several genres have a subsubheading of "Collections & Anthologies", thus lessening the need for multiple coding.

(See www.bisg.org/page/Fiction for the full list of categories.)

KDP, Draft2Digital, and Kobo Writing Life all include *Anthologies* and *Short Stories* as categories to which to assign a work, so be sure to use these as appropriate for your short fiction.

Resources

James Scott Bell's *How to Write Short Stories And Use Them to Further Your Writing Career* – Offers tips on set-up of short fiction on Amazon's KDP platform

LIBRARIES

When you publish standalone short story e-books through platforms like Draft2Digital or PublishDrive, you also have the option to include distribution to the various library wholesale platforms. This allows libraries to acquire your short stories and short story collections along with novels and books.

Libraries acquire a book using either a model known as OCOU (One Copy One User) or a special license called CPC (Cost Per Checkout).

The OCOU model works similarly to the way a library would acquire a physical book. When they purchase a single e-book, they can loan it out to one patron at a time. Once that patron is finished with that e-book and returns it, the library can loan it to a different patron. If the library wants to loan it to two patrons at the same time, they have to purchase a second copy of that e-book.

Some libraries opt for the CPC model where they don't actually purchase the book, but instead curate it into an online listing of selected titles that are presented as available to their patrons. When a patron checks out that book, the library pays the equivalent of roughly 10% of the book's purchase price.

This option allows the library to offer a broader selection of titles without immediately using up their funding, paying only for the books that patrons actually check out. While the pay is one tenth of a sale, the benefit to publishers and authors in this model is that they earn money for every single check out of that book. And after a book has been checked out more than ten times, the revenue surpasses what it would have earned on a single sale of that item. These micro-payments can add up over time.

As with sales of short fiction on retail sites, borrows by library patrons allow readers to get a taste for your writing style by sampling a shorter work while also adding to the multiple streams of revenue that feed your author business.

SERIALS AND SUBSCRIPTIONS

For short fiction authors, serialization offers a compelling way to build audience engagement, generate income, and expand a single story's lifespan. While serialization used to be the domain of magazines and newspapers, today's digital tools allow indie authors to publish stories in installments across a range of platforms.

Subscription platforms like Ream, Substack, and Patreon give authors flexibility in format, pricing, and audience interaction. With Substack, authors can serialize stories via email and web posts, building both a newsletter list and a paid subscriber base. Ream, a platform designed specifically for fiction authors, offers a tiered subscription model and tools for serial content delivery. Patreon functions similarly, with additional monetization features and optional community tools. Platforms like these provide income diversification, since they allow you to build a community of subscribers who support your work through ongoing payments while also engaging with your posts, updates, and discussions.

You might also consider self-serializing on your own website or through a newsletter, giving you full control over the content and the reader relationships. While this approach requires more setup and promotion, it can be an effective list- and brand-building strategy. Direct serialization helps authors strengthen their platform by driving readers to their own websites or mailing lists, where the author maintains full control of branding, data, and follow-up marketing opportunities. The key is to match your story structure, audience goals, and comfort with tech to the option that best supports your publishing strategy.

Here are some guidelines to follow to ensure your readers enjoy their experience with this type of offering.

- Consider what you are willing to commit to and position your offering accordingly. With a subscription for standalone stories—e.g., one story per month for subscribers—you could easily wrap up the subscription if the interest of you or your subscribers begins to wane. With a serial— i.e., each installment does not necessarily constitute a complete story and may end with a cliffhanger—you are committing to complete the overall story arc, and discontinuing the content mid-series is sure to anger your readers.
- Consider your creation versus publication strategy. For serial offerings, consider completing the serial before launching it to your subscribers; this way you know you will not disappoint them by flagging in mid-series. Standalone stories will give you more flexibility, but even with these, it's a good idea to have a number of stories completed before offering a subscription to readers. If you go to the trouble of setting up a subscription and then run out of ideas after a few stories, it will be a disappointment to your readers and to you.

- Set the expectation about the nature of your offering with your readers upfront. Especially with serials, use promotional material, product description, and even the work's sub-title to ensure the reader understands the serial nature of the offering. Also set the expectation with readers about the time over which the offering will play out. Especially with serials, you should plan to publish the installments over a relatively short period of time: days or weeks, not months. Readers will get frustrated if they have to wait too long for the full story to be completed.

- Divide the story so that if the reader purchases all the installments, they will pay a reasonable price for the whole experience. Don't publish a chapter-by-chapter serial with fifty installments, each selling for $0.99, and expect the reader to stick around for almost $50 worth of payments to get the whole story. Find some other way to divide the story; for example, perhaps the story takes place over five days, and each day is one installment costing $1.99.

CONTESTS

Short fiction contests provide another opportunity for short fiction authors. For winners, "award-winning author" is a great credential to include on your website and in your author bios. Cash prizes, sometimes even for short-listed works, are an additional source of revenue for your author business. Depending on the platform and how winning stories are presented—in an anthology, listed on a prestigious website or in a trade journal or magazine, or perhaps included on a platform that allows readers to enjoy the entire story—this is also an opportunity for increasing your author brand and SEO.

The perks provided to winners can be impressive. For example, the *Writers of the Future* contest grants prizes of $500, $750, and $1,000 every quarter for original science fiction, fantasy, and horror stories; winners' stories appear alongside those from the bestselling authors in the business; and winners are flown to spend a week in Los Angeles being mentored on the craft and business of writing by a stellar panel of judges. The week culminates in a black-tie celebration of the anthology and the announcement of the Grand Prize winner, who receives an additional $5,000.

As with any opportunity, there are a few disreputable short fiction contests out there among the many reputable ones, and here are a few red flags to watch out for:

- **High entry fees for low-value contests** – If the prize money or exposure doesn't reasonably match the cost to enter, the contest may be more about profiting from authors than rewarding them.
- **Fake or inflated prizes** – Some contests promise large cash awards or big promotional opportunities but either don't deliver them or exaggerate their worth to lure entrants.
- **Mandatory "winner" purchases** – Be wary of contests that require winners to buy copies of the anthology, certificates, or other merchandise in order to receive recognition.
- **Rights grabs in the fine print** – Unscrupulous contests may try to claim excessive or permanent rights to your work, preventing you from publishing or profiting from it elsewhere.
- **Phony endorsements or affiliations** – Some contests falsely claim ties to respected organizations, awards, or individuals in order to appear legitimate when they're not.

For information about what goes on behind the scenes of reputable contests, and how you can stack the odds in your favor, see the chapter "Behind the Curtain: Insights from the Curator's Desk" in the **Best Practices** section.

AUDIO

With the explosion of interest in audiobooks and the developing focus on audio-first publishing, don't overlook audio for your short fiction for income creation opportunities. New services and offerings are popping up across the industry to meet authors' desire to make audio a viable medium for their short fiction.

The biggest name in indie audiobook production, Amazon's ACX, is probably not an option for short fiction for the reasons described below, but platforms such as Voices by INaudio (formerly Findaway Voices) is filling this gap.

Production

One option for short fiction audio is to narrate and produce the audiobook yourself. The shorter length makes the time commitment more manageable, and you can better maintain consistent voice performance than you might with a longer project. But consider that listeners expect not just a reading but a performance of the work, and acting is a different skill than writing. Will you be able to provide a performance that will be compelling for listeners? Mark's theater experience stands him in good stead when narrating his own short fiction.

Advances in technology have made high-quality recording equipment more affordable than ever, and user-friendly editing software now enables even beginners to produce professional results.

For those with the right skill set, narrating and producing your own audiobook shorts usually means lower costs and faster payback (as always, remember to assign a value to your time).

But perhaps hiring a professional narrator seems like a better choice. You can find narrators through platforms such as Amazon ACX or Voices.com, where you can search and filter on criteria like rates, genres, styles, and regional accents and listen to voice samples. The most common payment arrangement for short fiction is a per finished hour rate (with payment based on the final length of the work, not the time the narrator spends creating the audio), so short fiction can be a cost-effective entry point for authors interested in audio. (Royalty share agreements are uncommon for short fiction due to lower earning potential than with novel-length works.)

You might also look for narrators through writing and voice-over communities, or even through local acting groups or drama schools. Consider engaging a newer narrator who is building their portfolio and is open to smaller-scale work.

Narrators often handle both the narration and the production of the audiobook—for example, ensuring the final audio meets the technical specifications required by distribution platforms—but be sure your contract explicitly includes this service if you expect it.

Distribution

Indie publishing on Amazon's ACX makes the audiobook available on Amazon, Apple, and Audible, which represents more than half of the U.S. audiobook market. However, the challenge with distributing short fiction audio via ACX is that ACX, not the author, assigns the price, and they are not likely to price short fiction low enough in comparison to novel-length works to make them attractive to listeners. In addition, Audible members acquire many of their audiobooks through monthly credits, and they are not likely to use a credit on a half-hour short fiction audiobook if they can use the same credit for a book of a dozen hours or more. Furthermore, ACX's control of pricing means that authors can't adjust pricing for promotional purposes, especially painful in view of BookBub's launch of Chirp as a marketing tool for discounted audiobooks.

Consider that if you have a collection of audio shorts, then assembling them into a collection whose overall length is more comparable to novel-length works might make a platform like ACX more viable.

For individual short story audio, distributors like Voices by INaudio and Author's Republic are better options. They enable authors to set the price of their audiobooks, allowing for the possibility of doing special price-drop promotions.

Library Lending

Short fiction authors can make their audiobooks available for libraries to acquire through platforms like OverDrive, Bibliotheca, Hoopla, and Odilo. All of these platforms can be reached via either Voices by INaudio or Author's Republic. (ACX does not support library lending of audiobooks, which is a growing income opportunity for authors.) See the "Libraries" chapter for more information.

Payback

The more formats you offer—print, e-book, audio—the more likely you are to have the one that appeals to any particular reader or listener, and therefore to make the sale. And you also open up the possibility that a reader / listener will purchase one work in multiple formats.

That said, audio typically has the longest payback period of any format, so you may want to test reader interest in your short fiction through e-book and print editions before investing in audio production. Mark started investing in audiobook production back in 2014, and interestingly, the first works on which he earned back his investment were individual short stories and mini story collections, often through the micro-payments of CPC (Cost Per Checkout) as discussed in the "Libraries" chapter.

AI Narration – Yea or Nay?

Any discussion of audio would be incomplete without a note about AI narration, although our note will be brief. The state of the industry is changing so quickly that any information we provided here about AI-generated audio production and distribution platforms would quickly become out of date. Those changes mean that the difference in experience for the listeners between AI and human narration will become smaller over time. We both offer AI-narrated audio versions of our nonfiction books, but as of this writing, we believe that even the most advanced AI tools cannot match the richness and nuance of a skilled human narrator. We recommend that, if at all possible, you work with a human narrator for your short fiction.

Resources

Voice by INaudio (formerly Findaway Voices) (https://www.inaudio.com/)

Author's Republic – From Author's Republic's website: "Author's Republic is more than just an audiobook publisher. We're a new solution for getting your audiobook onto more platforms and in front of more listeners in the easiest way ever." (www.authorsrepublic.com/)

Chirp – BookBub's audiobook promotion platform (https://www.chirpbooks.com/home)

PATRON SUPPORT

Have you ever enjoyed a piece of free content—a podcast, a blog, an online article—whose creator you felt deserved some compensation for his or her work? There are services that enable committed fans to provide such financial support, a few of which we describe below.

Membership Services

Patreon is a membership service that enables those who benefit from the output of creators to provide financial support through small monthly payments. For example, Patreon supporters might support a public podcast with a few dollars a month and in return receive access to a private podcast or other special content. This is a model that we both use for our podcasts, *The Indy Author Podcast* and *Stark Reflections on Writing and Publishing*.

The same model can be used to earn money from your short fiction. You might commit to providing subscribers with a new piece of short fiction each month in text, audio, or video format.

Keep in mind that Patreon is not designed to help you find

new readers—it works best once you've already built a following through other channels.

(Reference the chapter "Serials and Subscriptions" for ways you can use short fiction on a membership platform like Patreon.)

e-Commerce Donation

There are other options available to enable fans to reward you financially for your work, even when it's available to them for free. Matty uses one such service, Buy Me a Coffee, to enable supporters to acknowledge the value of her work through small (and sometimes large) contributions. You can link to such services on any web page where you are offering content—but do it in a subtle way so as not to alienate your followers. Matty puts her Buy Me a Coffee button in the footer of her website, which is both non-intrusive and easy to direct people to ("Just go to the bottom of any page at TheIndyAuthor.com and click Buy Me a Coffee to make a small contribution").

Crowdfunding

Crowdfunding platforms such as Kickstarter and Indiegogo offer short fiction authors an opportunity to fund projects through reader support, as well as to earn some extra income beyond the amount needed for the project. Short stories can play a key role in these campaigns, especially since their short length makes them easier to produce quickly and to offer in multiple formats (e-book, print chapbook, audio), adding flexibility to your campaign design.

Short fiction might be the primary focus of your campaign— for example, to fund a special edition collection of shorts. But short fiction is often used as bonus rewards in conjunction with other offerings: for example, using a piece of short fiction or a collection of shorts as an early reward in a campaign that will culminate with a longer work, perhaps a novel featuring the protagonist of your short stories. You might also offer a stretch goal involving short fiction—for example, the commitment to write a new short story set in the world of the novel on offer if the campaign reaches a certain threshold.

Because short fiction can be delivered digitally with little to no fulfillment cost, it's particularly well suited to low-tier pledge levels. This helps you build momentum without taking on logistical complexity. If you've already written or published short stories, including them in a campaign lets you leverage existing assets in a way that deepens reader engagement and increases the value of your offerings.

And crowdfunding campaigns can serve your reader connection goals as well, since platforms like Kickstarter are increasingly becoming a discovery platform as well as a patronage platform.

Resources

Patreon – A membership platform that enables supporters to provide financial support to creators (www.patreon.com/)

Buy Me a Coffee (www.buymeacoffee.com/) and tiny-Coffee (www.wpplugindirectory.org/tinycoffee/) – Enable supporters to provide financial support to creators

FOREIGN LANGUAGE MARKETS

Although the English language short fiction market is an obvious choice for English language authors, huge opportunities exist elsewhere. For example, Asia is a flourishing short fiction market. If you follow the advice of Douglas Smith, author of *Playing the Short Game: How to Market and Sell Short Fiction*, any money you earn from foreign markets will be found money on top of already-earned money from English-language outlets. In his article "Selling to Foreign Language Markets," Smith offers this important caveat to foreign market sales: only submit a story to foreign language markets once you have sold it to an English-language market.

Many of the top English language genre fiction markets have foreign language editions or will ask for an option on foreign language rights. Selling a story to a non-English market first could jeopardize a more prestigious and lucrative English first-rights sale. In addition, it's a lot easier to sell to a foreign language market if your story has the credentials of a major English-language market.

If you receive an offer from a foreign language market, pay special attention to the arrangement for distributing payments to ensure that, for example, payment via bank transfer doesn't carry fees that will significantly eat into your earnings from that work.

You can enjoy follow-on income benefits by the discoverability that a foreign language placement will provide with that market, as noted by Kristine Kathryn Rusch:

A lot of book publishers read short fiction in translation, searching for that great writer from another country. Some organizations in those countries give awards for best translated work, including short stories. If you have a good translation and your story gets nominated, you will come to the attention of that country's publishers. They'll consider your work without telling you. So you won't know if you've been rejected by them. But they will contact you if they're interested in publishing one of your novels.

—Kristine Kathryn Rusch, "Subsidiary Rights for Indies"

You don't need to find a translator to take advantage of foreign market opportunities; markets exist that will take on the responsibility of translating short fiction into other languages.

As with audiobook narration, a discussion of translation would not be complete without some consideration of the use of AI. While we do have extensive experience using AI-generated audiobook narration, we have only recently begun exploring the use of this technology when it comes to translated works. In addition, the state of the technology is evolving so rapidly that any assessment made of its capabilities today would quickly be out of date.

For example, during our work on this second edition of *Taking the Short Tack*, Mark began working with Scribe-Shadow, a company that specializes in AI translations about which native speakers have offered high praise and near 5-star rating averages. Mark used ScribeShadow to translate his short story "This Time Around," part of his *Canadian Werewolf* series, and beta readers told him that the translation is solid and effective. And ScribeShadow was even able to provide an optimized French version of the title (not a literal translation): "Encore Une Fois : Une Histoire de Loup-Garou Canadien." "Encore une fois" means "one more time," which reflects the essence of the story, in which the main character must deal with the challenges he faces while transforming from man to wolf and back in New York City.

Mark's use of knowledgeable beta readers to review the translation is key: never share a piece of AI-translated work without first running it by a human who is fluent in the translated language. (AI translation is one area where we anticipate that the technology might expand human job opportunities rather than reduce them, since professional authors who might never otherwise pursue translations will be looking for qualified editors to vet their AI-generated translations.)

You can find foreign language market rights via sites like Duotrope and Submittable, but also through Douglas Smith's Foreign Market List.

Keep your sights on all global markets to increase the money-earning potential of each of your short works.

Resources

Douglas Smith Article: Selling to Foreign Markets (www.smith writer.com/FML_article)

Douglas Smith's Foreign Market List (www.smithwriter.com/foreign_market_list.htm)

Kristine Kathryn Rusch, "Subsidiary Rights for Indies" (https://kriswrites.com/2017/10/11/business-musings-subsidiary-rights-for-indies/)

ScribeShadow – AI-powered translation (https://www.scribeshadow.com/)

GETTING UNSTUCK

As Matty was exploring the ways that the nautical concept of the short tack works well as a metaphor for short fiction, she uncovered this: "If your engine dies one day—and you can bet it will—the ability to 'short-tack' could be vital to know."

That suggested one additional use to which you might put short fiction.

Ever been in the midst of a novel and hit a wall—had your creative engine die? We all have. You can continue to try to force your way forward, doing the authorial equivalent of fiddling with a clogged fuel filter or whacking the engine with your wrench. However, at some point you need to acknowledge that, at that moment, the engine of long-form inspiration is not going to carry you forward.

No one earns income from a story that isn't getting written, so what do you do?

Try switching to a short story.

Short stories don't carry the same authorial baggage as a novel, so you can approach them in a more lighthearted manner. As Lawrence Block says in *The Liar's Companion: A Field Guide for Fiction Writers*, "I figured short stories would be fun.

They always are. I think I probably enjoy them more than novels. When they go well, they provide almost immediate gratification. When they go horribly hopelessly wrong, so what? To discard a failed short story is to throw away the work of a handful of hours, perhaps a couple of days. In a short story I can try new things, play with new styles, and take unaccustomed risks. They're fun."

Step back from the work whose engine has died and take a short tack with a piece of short fiction to get your voyage—and your income-earning potential—moving forward again.

Resources

The Indy Author Podcast:

Episode 164 - What Writers Can Learn from Short Fiction with Gabriela Pereira

Episode 192 - Stretching Your Writing Muscles with Short Fiction with Richie Narvaez

PART 3

CONNECTING WITH READERS

INTRODUCTION - CONNECTING WITH READERS

Creating connections is one of the primary reasons that humans create stories. Jimmy Neil Smith, founder and president emeritus of the International Storytelling Center, says, "We are all storytellers. We all live in a network of stories. There isn't a stronger connection between people than storytelling." Peter Forbes of the Center for Whole Communities argues that "stories create community."

You can use your work to create your own community of readers who will love what you have to offer them.

This section, **Connecting with Readers**, may be most applicable to writers who are primarily interested in leveraging short fiction to support their full-length book projects or to expose new readers to their work (versus the **Creating Income** section, which may be more applicable to authors who are primarily short fiction writers). However, it's worth reviewing both sections regardless of what your goals are, because a concept that we categorize as related to creating income may trigger ideas for reader outreach and vice versa.

You can use short fiction to connect with readers who are unfamiliar with your work; Mark has created multiple mini chapbooks of themed short stories as hooks into some of his full-length books. You can also use short fiction to maintain a connection with readers who are already familiar with your work; Matty wrote the Ann Kinnear Suspense Shorts as a way to tide over her Ann fans while she worked on her first three Lizzy Ballard Thrillers.

The *short* of short fiction means these works can be produced more quickly than long-form fiction and so enable more frequent releases and the resultant marketing benefits of staying front-of-mind with your followers.

Short fiction can also serve as a "business card" for other endeavors, such as editing services, since it is a concise way of connecting with potential clients by giving them a sample of your work.

In this section on **Connecting with Readers**, we will address:

- **Offering Your Story for Free** – Providing readers with free access to your short fiction through various platforms and promotions
- **Reader Funnel** – Reaching new readers by offering low-priced or free short fiction as an introduction to your world, characters, or writing style
- **Reader Magnet** – Encouraging readers who enjoy your work to stay connected through a platform you control, such as your author newsletter
- **Video** – Sharing your short fiction in an engaging, visual format to capture attention and connect with readers
- **Author Readings** – Introducing your short fiction to new audiences through live readings

- **Market Research** – Testing a story, character, or world in short fiction format before committing to a longer work
- **Flash Fiction and Micro-Fiction** – Leveraging ultra-short formats to create marketing and promotional opportunities, especially on social media
- **Chapbooks** – Publishing short fiction in small-format print books traditionally used for poetry
- **Bonus Material** – Strengthening reader connections by including a piece of short fiction as a bonus with a longer work
- **Custom Story** – Creating personalized short fiction as a unique offering for individual readers or patrons
- **Location-Based Apps** – Connecting your short fiction to specific geographic locations through interactive platforms
- **When the Reader Is an Agent** – Using short fiction publications to build your résumé and attract industry professionals
- **As a Gift** – Creating a personalized short story as a meaningful and unique gift

OFFERING YOUR STORY FOR FREE

Using your short fiction as a means of connecting with readers usually means finding a way to get your story to the reader for free, so we begin this section with a description of a few of the means available to do this. These options will apply to a number of strategies and tactics described in this **Connecting with Readers** section.

Before making your short story available for free, take time to consider your goals for connecting with readers. Many authors offer free content not just to get their story in front of readers, but to serve a broader purpose such as sparking interest in a story world or character that leads to other paid offerings or inviting readers into a deeper relationship through a newsletter or membership. Be sure your free offering aligns with your long-term goals for your books and your author career.

Retail Sites

Most online retail sites—Apple Books, Barnes & Noble, Kobo— allow you to set the price to zero for an unlimited period of time.

It's trickier with Amazon. There are two scenarios for achieving a price of $0.00 on Amazon.

If you are in **KDP Select**—i.e., if your book is available exclusively on Amazon—then Amazon will allow you to price it at $0.00 *for a limited number of days over a specified amount of time* (up to five days out of each 90-day KDP Select enrollment period).

If you are **NOT in KDP Select**—i.e., your book is available on other platforms such as Apple Books, Barnes & Noble, Kobo, or your direct sales store —then the lowest price you can set directly via the KDP tools is $0.99. The only way to get Amazon to set the price to $0.00 is to set it to zero on the other platforms and then contact **KDP Support** directly (via the "Contact Us" option in your KDP dashboard) with links to the free listings, requesting that Amazon price-match.

This is not a foolproof method. For example, your book could be free on Amazon for a time and then get bumped back up in price. Amazon might price match in some markets but not others—for example, Amazon will price match in the US and UK but not in Canada, Australia, Italy, or Germany. And you will only discover this if you monitor the Amazon listing across all the markets. When advertising your free offering, it's wise to include the caveat that it is free on *most* retail platforms to allow for this geographic differential, and to check your home market listing periodically.

Downloadable Files

You can post a downloadable file on your website, and directing people there for your free offering may increase the likelihood that they will also sign up for your e-mail list, especially if you use a well-designed, non-intrusive pop-up to encourage that.

However, posting an epub file can invite technical support

headaches from readers unfamiliar with sideloading e-books onto their devices. Offering a pdf is simpler on your end, but the experience is less seamless and less enjoyable for readers who prefer reading on dedicated e-readers or apps.

A better solution is to use a service that handles file delivery and support for you. Two popular and author-friendly options are BookFunnel and StoryOrigin.

BookFunnel is a subscription service that provides you with a customizable landing page where readers can download your story in multiple formats (e.g., epub, pdf, and audio). You can also password-protect the page to limit access to specific readers. BookFunnel delivers a polished, professional experience and removes the burden of tech support from your shoulders.

StoryOrigin offers similar functionality, including file delivery, landing pages, and email list integration. It also provides tools for newsletter swaps, review tracking, and reader magnets—making it a strong all-in-one platform for authors looking to grow and engage their audience. It even offers a free plan.

Resources

BookFunnel (www.bookfunnel.com/)
StoryOrigin (https://storyoriginapp.com/)

READER FUNNEL

A reader funnel can help you reach readers who are not yet familiar with your work by offering them free material as an introduction to your world, your characters, and your writing style. Unlike a reader magnet, discussed in the next chapter, the reader funnel does not require the reader to take any prerequisite action such as signing up for a mailing list before receiving the free work.

Origin stories, character backstories, and prequels all work well as reader funnels. Mark offers a short story called "Prospero's Ghost" as a free standalone e-book on all the major retailers. It is a story that appears in an anthology he edited called *Campus Chills*.

For a piece of short fiction to act successfully as a funnel to other work, you must select your material appropriately. "Prospero's Ghost" is an effective funnel to *Campus Chills* because it offers an example of the type of horror tale that appears in the anthology. A sweet romance short story, no matter how well written, will not be an effective reader funnel if the works to which it leads readers are in the horror genre. You won't make any sales, and you will likely receive a lot of angry e-mails.

The short work you are using as a funnel doesn't necessarily need to encompass the same characters or worlds as your other works, but it needs to set an accurate expectation with the reader about your genre and style.

In addition to setting the right expectations for your other works, it's also important that a piece of short fiction used as a reader funnel or as a reader magnet provides a self-contained story arc and that the reader will be satisfied even if they don't proceed to the longer work. Otherwise you risk making a foe rather than a friend or a potential fan.

Also consider whether the story requires the reader to have knowledge of another of your works to fully appreciate it. If it does not, it will make a good reader **funnel** because you want to expose readers to new books that will appeal to them. If it does, it might make a better reader **magnet** (reference the chapter "Reader Magnet").

If your piece of short fiction forms a part of the longer work to which you are directing readers, make sure to include a note to that effect at the end of the short work. For example, Mark's short story *This Time Around* includes a note that the story constitutes, in somewhat modified form, the first three chapters of a longer work, *A Canadian Werewolf in New York* along with a link to the full-length novel.

Mark's cover design also indicates the related nature of these two works by using similar images on both.

Also consider how the storyline of your short fiction is or is not consistent with or tied to your other works—for example, novels that involve the same cast of characters. Matty tries to avoid any references that would encourage a reader to try to place the Ann Kinnear Suspense Shorts in a timeline along with the Ann Kinnear Suspense Novels. Because a short story might one day become a novel, perhaps with some major plot adjustments, she positions the short stories as a separate but parallel world.

If you choose to place the short work in a storyline along

with the novels of the series, then a timeline of the chronology could be a fun bonus to provide for fans on your website or as a reader magnet.

No matter where and how you distribute your short story, be sure to set the expectation with the reader that it's short fiction and not a novel. This might mean providing an explicit call-out in the work's sub-title (e.g., "The Ann Kinnear Suspense Shorts") as well as in the online product description.

For a piece of short fiction to succeed as a funnel to other works, you must make sure it's easy for the reader to get to those other works, so be sure to include links to your other works at the end of the reader funnel (and, in fact, at the end of any piece of work you publish). Reference the chapter "Links and QR Codes" in the **Best Practices** section for more information.

READER MAGNET

A reader magnet is an offering that encourages readers to stay in touch via a platform you control.

We strongly recommend against relying on retail platforms like Amazon and Barnes & Noble or on social media platforms to stay in touch with your fans. The rules those players impose, and even the players themselves, can change without warning, leaving you cut off from the people who most want to stay in touch with you. The most common and consistently shared advice in the author community is to have your own e-mail list, a platform that is completely within your control.

But how do you attract readers to your list? The promise to tell them what you're up to and when you're launching a new book may not be enough. It's important to offer potential subscribers more, and a free story, especially if it ties in with your purchasable books, is a perfect magnet.

Authors might consider offering an entire book for free as a reader magnet; this is a technique that works quite effectively, particularly if the author has a lot of assets available. But you risk attracting only readers for whom price (i.e., free) is the first consideration when choosing a book. These are not the people you want on your mailing list—they can actually cost you money if you are using an e-mail service that charges based on number of subscribers.

How might you use a piece of short fiction to alleviate this problem? Since the miserly reader is looking for the maximum amount of content for the minimum amount of effort (i.e., signing up for your mailing list and then, no doubt, directing your e-mails to their spam folder as soon as they've received the free offering), then they may be less likely to sign up for a short work.

The people who will take the time to sign up—and stay on your mailing list—are the people who are interested in your genre, your work, your world, or you personally.

Origin stories, character backstories, and prequel stories all work well as reader magnets. If a reader has fallen in love with a character in your novel, the idea that they can learn more about that character through your reader magnet short story or vignette will be a compelling offer. True fans want the Easter egg tales, those extra elements that highlight a character they loved or extend a story with a "director's cut" version. They'll enjoy seeing a secondary character from a longer work take center stage in a reader magnet that explores their story more deeply. They revel in the value of that experience rather than thinking of it merely as free content.

Consider expanding your reader reach by partnering with another author to coauthor a short story that features both of your protagonists. Matty did this after discovering that the protagonist of fellow Sisters in Crime author Jane Gorman's novels—Philadelphia Police Detective Adam Kaminski—shared a last name with the ex-boyfriend of Ann Kinnear, the protagonist of Matty's suspense series. That coincidence sparked the idea for a collaboration, and the result was *Blood of the Wicked*, a short story in which Adam and Ann team up to investigate a crime in Philadelphia—a city that serves as the backdrop for both authors' books. Each author shared the story with their own audience, introducing their readers to a new character and a new author in the process. Coauthored reader magnets work best when the authors' styles and story worlds are compatible—for example, when both write in similar genres and share a comparable tone: gritty or cozy, humorous or dark. This ensures a seamless experience for readers and increases the likelihood that fans of one author will become fans of the other.

You could also consider using deleted scenes as a reader magnet since, as with movie watchers, readers of one of your novels will enjoy finding out what got left on the cutting room floor. Matty has found that a side benefit of this is that it takes some of the sting out of axing a scene from your novel-in-progress if you know you will be able to use it as a reader magnet.

Consider whether the work requires the reader to have knowledge of another of your works to fully appreciate it. If it does, it will make a good reader **magnet**. It will encourage people who have already experienced your work to engage with you more actively, for example by signing up for your e-mail list. If it does not require knowledge of your other works, then it might make a better reader **funnel** because you want to expose those readers to new books that will appeal to them (reference the chapter "Reader Funnel").

By using a piece of short fiction as a reader magnet, you not only ensure that you control the means of communicating with your fans by building a robust e-mail list but also tease them with a glimpse into your stories and your characters to ensure that they are as excited as you are when your next book comes out.

VIDEO

Video can provide attention-getting and engaging ways of sharing your work and connecting with readers.

Consider reading your work on a live online video event, such as Instagram or Facebook Live, or post a video on YouTube.

For an example of using videos of readings of short works, check out Mark's videos at www.markleslie.ca/freefri dayfrights/ or search for *mark leslie free friday frights*. Every Friday, Mark aired a live video in which he read a short story or shared a tale related to one of his non-fiction ghost stories. After reading or discussing the piece, he would share a bit of background on the story or the research involved in its creation.

The intent behind this weekly effort was to entice people who weren't already familiar with Mark's writing to check out his stories. It also increased the search engine optimization, or SEO, related to Mark's fiction, via an increase in followers on Facebook and an increase in YouTube subscribers. He also saw a small but noticeable bump in traffic to his website based on search results related to keywords from the title and metadata descriptions and tags used for those posts. There are now dozens of videos on Facebook and YouTube that, even years afterward, continue to bring Mark's work to the attention of new readers.

You can employ these suggestions for video to audio offerings as well. Performing an audio-only reading of your short fiction and publishing it via an RSS feed or a podcast or on YouTube can be a similar discoverability tool that helps attract new readers to your universe. And because viewer or listener expectations are different for these more informal, free offerings, you don't need to deliver pro-level products (although the experience of recording your work might provide an indication of whether you're a candidate for narrating or performing your work as a paid offering).

If your work is traditionally published, be sure to consider what your agreement with your publisher will allow. Since Mark had licensed the rights to many of his non-fiction stories in books such as *Creepy Capital*, *Haunted Hamilton*, *Haunted Hospitals*, and *Tomes of Terror* to a traditional publisher, he couldn't read the stories in full in his online video series. He opted instead to discuss the tales from those chapters so as not to violate the terms of his contract. This is a great example of how you can leverage your intellectual property by drawing on the source research used to create a specific piece. Even if the work is not in your control, you can generate new and original content derived from or inspired by that same source content and still be compliant with the terms and conditions of your contract.

AUTHOR READINGS

Author readings are a great way to introduce your work to people who might not otherwise find you, especially since readings are often themed (e.g., noir, humor) and therefore draw a crowd that is already interested in that genre. Authors are often able to sell their books at these events and so have the potential for income creation. However, book sales are by no means guaranteed, especially if you find yourself reading to the same audience time after time (as you may at readings sponsored by a particular writers' group). Therefore, we have categorized readings as mainly a reader connection opportunity.

Readers are generally limited to five to ten minutes which, assuming a reading rate of 175 words per minute, equates to 875 to 1,750 words. (Never try to squeeze in more content by reading faster—the audience won't be able to appreciate your work. Never blow past the time limit that organizers have set— they won't appreciate your attitude, and you are likely not to get a repeat invitation.)

Authors will often read an excerpt from a longer work, and they benefit from the opportunity to entice the audience with a teaser in the hopes that they will buy the longer work. However, using a piece of short fiction that you can read in its entirety within the proscribed time has the advantage of giving the audience a complete story arc. And you can enjoy the same benefit in terms of potential sales by having available for sale a chapbook or print anthology that contains the story you read. You could even offer a printout of the text of the reading that includes the names of your other works, plus QR codes to link readers to online sites where they can purchase those works. (Reference the "Links and QR Codes" chapter in the **Best Practices** section for more information.)

Mark has long used his short story "That Old Silk Hat They Found" for author readings. This is a *Twilight Zone*-style tale about what might happen if a snowman came to life. Running about 1,800 words, this tale is humorous and, although dark, is appropriate for listeners of all ages. It also features multiple voices which, performed effectively, provides additional entertainment value for the audience. Mark's readings of "That Old Silk Hat They Found" regularly result in sales of Mark's short story collections.

Participation in readings can also pay off by enabling you to connect not only with readers but also with fellow authors. By using these events as networking opportunities, you expand your connections within the writing and publishing communities and the support those communities can provide: authors with whom you can exchange editing or proofreading services, editors / curators through whom you may learn of anthology opportunities, and more.

Resources

For an in-depth discussion of the best practices for author readings, check out the book Matty coauthored with M.L. Ronn, *From Page to Platform: How to Succeed as an Author Speaker.*

MARKET RESEARCH

In the days before computer-aided design, when boat builders were developing a new craft, they would create a small-scale model, letting them quickly assess stability, performance, and appearance in a fast-to-create, easy-to-iterate proxy before committing to the full-scale build. If towing the model showed the bow throwing too much spray, the builder might reshape the front to slice the water more cleanly. If the model wouldn't hold a straight line, they might reconfigure the hull.

A short story works the same way for writers.

Do you have a story, character, or world in mind but want to try it out before committing months or even years to develop it into a novel-length work? Try it first as a piece of short fiction and see if it resonates with readers ... and if it resonates with *you.*

This use works best if you already have a following with whom you can conduct this proof-of-concept experiment. For example, Mark originally wrote the short stories "This Time Around" and "I, Death" not intending to expand them beyond their original format, but once his fans read them, they demanded that Mark provide novel-length treatments.

Similarly, when Mark finished the first draft of his novel *Evasion* during NaNoWriMo (National Novel Writing Month) 2013, he posted it to Wattpad with a prefatory note to readers that it was an uncorrected and unedited first draft that he was sharing to gauge reader response.

While this was a work of about 55,000 words and therefore not short fiction by our definitions, the intent was the same: market research that Mark used to help him determine next steps for that particular piece of content.

When the feedback came in, the response was overwhelming. Not only did the readers love the story, but they asked where they could buy it in e-book and print. They wanted to know if there would be a sequel, because they really enjoyed the main character and wanted to read more about him. It wasn't long before Mark dedicated resources toward re-writing and publishing the book, making it available in e-book, print, and audio. He could invest that time knowing that the work already had an eager audience.

Matty is considering spinning off a secondary character from her Lizzy Ballard Thrillers into a series of his own and plans to test the concept's viability by starting with a few short stories.

You can use short fiction not only to market test your work in advance of a longer treatment, or in advance of making the effort to publish it in various formats, but also to gain valuable marketing insights into your audience. Storytelling platforms such as Wattpad, which is focused on community-building rather than outright marketing, do nonetheless provide you with invaluable data about your readers, including gender, age, and geographical location, and you can leverage this information when planning marketing and promotion campaigns. Having this type of data can reduce your expenses, ensuring that you are focusing your marketing and advertising dollars as efficiently as possible by connecting with the readers who will most appreciate your work.

FLASH FICTION AND MICRO-FICTION

Flash fiction is generally defined as a story of fewer than a thousand words and micro-fiction fewer than three hundred words—in some cases, far fewer (case in point: the story ascribed to Hemingway: "For sale: baby shoes, never worn.").

Flash fiction and micro-fiction offer especially intriguing marketing and promotion opportunities in this age of social media. In fact, Mark sold the following micro-story to a Twitter platform called *Tweet the Meat*:

"It wasn't me," Carl said, "my shadow killed him."

The detective smiled. "Your Shadow will rot in prison. But we need you to keep it there."

(Although Mark received one of his highest per-word payouts for this story, you can imagine why we're not suggesting flash fiction or micro-fiction as primarily a money-making opportunity.)

In February 2023, Dan Willcocks and Sam Frost of the Activated Authors community set out a challenge to writers. They offered twenty-eight prompts over twenty-eight days with a daily deadline for writers to write and submit a piece of flash fiction. From the over five hundred stories submitted, they selected 77 of the best to include in a 2024 anthology entitled *Bolts of Fiction: A Flash Fiction Anthology*. Mark followed a half dozen of these prompts and submitted a few of them to the project. Two of his stories were accepted for publication. And he also now has a handful of other micro-fiction pieces he can leverage.

Flash or micro-fiction can also offer opportunities for interaction with your followers on social media. Over the years many poets have leveraged platforms like Instagram for showing off their talent. It may work the same for pieces of micro-fiction. Consider posting a hyper-short story on a specified topic and invite your followers to post their own.

Use of flash or micro-fiction can also move beyond the electronic world. Consider using a micro-story—like Mark's "Carl's Shadow" story—on a postcard to be sent to bookstores to entice them to take a look at your longer works.

On top of the reader connection opportunities of flash and micro-fiction, they also offer a great opportunity for honing your craft, and for exercising that inner editor that makes sure that every word counts.

Resources

Stark Reflections on Writing and Publishing Episode 366 – Bolts of Fiction with Daniel Willcocks and Sam Frost - https://starkreflections.ca/2024/06/15/episode-366-bolts-of-fiction-with-daniel-willcocks-and-sam-frost/

The Indy Author Podcast Episode 098 - Redefining Indy Success through Short Fiction with Ran Walker

Generally the resources we mention are focused on the business of short fiction, but we can't resist including a recommendation for Ran Walker's charming *One Hundred Ways: A Handbook for Writing 100-Word Stories*, which, appropriately enough, is comprised of one hundred hundred-word chapters.

CHAPBOOKS

Another medium for short fiction is the chapbook. A chapbook is a small print book that is often used for poetry but that also lends itself nicely to short fiction. The chapbook might be a single story or a collection.

Chapbooks can provide income creation opportunities. Having a low-priced chapbook to offer at a conference or book fair may net you a sale from someone who isn't ready to make the investment for a full-length novel. A price of $5.00 is low enough to qualify as an impulse buy—certainly more so than most novel-length print books. You can also maximize income generation by adding QR codes linking to your purchasable books in your print chapbooks; reference the "Links and QR Codes" chapter in the **Best Practices** section for more information about QR codes.

However, we've chosen to position chapbooks as more focused on connecting with readers and on laying the groundwork for generating income from other works.

For example, you could make your primary income generators even more attractive by offering book fair customers a free chapbook if they purchase two of your books.

You might also consider a chapbook as a giveaway in order to acquaint readers with your work. A chapbook can function as an elegant "business card" to distribute judiciously at conferences. It not only displays your fiction-writing prowess but can also provide information on your other works, awards or kudos, and contact information.

The chapbook format is especially valuable in situations where you want to ensure that readers have easy access to your work. Mark created a chapbook of one of his short stories in the run-up to the Canadian Aurora Awards in order to address the requirement that people voting for the awards must have read the nominee's work. Providing the free print copy not only helped Mark expand the number of voters who met this requirement, but also created goodwill, because what reader doesn't love being given a free story, no matter the length?

Match the Production to the Goal

Chapbooks can be produced with varying levels of professionalism and polish—match the time and financial investment in their production to your intended purpose.

For example, a homemade chapbook might be fine as a bonus item you add to the bag of a reader who has purchased your novel at an in-person event, but it won't appeal to someone if you are asking them to pay for it. A book printed at your local office supply store could be professional-looking, but it won't be available via the regular online book retail platforms.

The minimum page count for the major distributors is surprisingly low: 24 pages for Amazon's KDP Print, 18 pages for IngramSpark, and 32 pages for Draft2Digital Print. (These very low page counts don't accommodate spine text.)

Mark has used Draft2Digital Print to create numerous chapbooks for single stories and mini story collections (example below). One of the benefits of their service is that it will make a machine-perfect full-wrap cover for the book using a front-cover image, with the ability to manually customize the text on the back cover and spine (if the page count is large enough to allow for spine text). This eliminates the costs associated with paying a designer to generate a full wraparound cover for the print book.

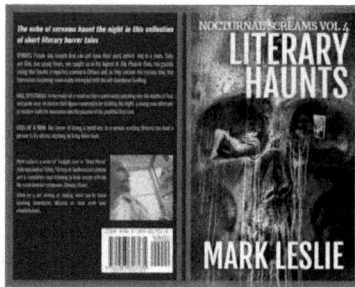

Matty created a chapbook of her Ann Kinnear Suspense Short "Write in Water," and to meet the printer's minimum page count requirement, she added an AI-created pen-and-ink image as a frontispiece and an Author's Note; even if these had not been needed to increase the page count, these additions made the offering even more appealing to readers.

Creating your chapbook on one of these platforms will provide professional quality and purchasability, but calculate the costs, including shipping if you are planning to order your own stock from a non-local printer, to appropriately match your goal with your cost for producing it.

BONUS MATERIAL

Another use to which you can put your short fiction to build reader connections through goodwill is to include it as bonus material in conjunction with a longer work. It's fun for readers to get to the end of a novel and discover they have a little more from that author's world to enjoy. For example, the audiobook of *Night of the Hidden Fang* by T. James Logan contains a bonus short story "Fangs in the Dark" involving characters that appear in the series.

A piece of short fiction can not only be used as bonus material itself but can also be the *subject* of bonus material. For example, consider providing author notes at the end of your short story, novelette, or novella—the fiction equivalent of behind-the-scenes material on a DVD. Mark includes these types of notes to provide information of interest to the story reader, such as where the inspiration for the story came from or background about the story's setting in time or place. In his mini story collection *Snowman Shivers: Two Dark Humor Tales About Snowmen*, Mark not only includes notes about each of the two stories featured in this collection, but he also has a bonus essay called "A Look at Anthropomorphic Snow Sculptures: A Brief History of Snowmen" where he shares historical trivia and a look at the use of snowmen in popular culture over the years.

This is largely a reader connection strategy because it's a way of deepening your relationship with the reader, but it could also be an income strategy if your notes lead readers to other works that share a similar inspiration or setting.

CUSTOM STORY

We have discussed how you can contribute a piece of short fiction to an anthology to support a good cause as a way of connecting with readers and building goodwill. Another way you can do your bit to be a good citizen of the author community—and your community at large—is through a custom story.

Mark has "killed" people for a few hundred dollars.

He used this technique to support the Hamilton Literacy Council. The council advertised in the local newspaper that Mark would write a story in which he killed off the contributor for a certain level of donation to the organization. Mark met with the contributor to collect some information with which to personalize the story and then wrote a custom short story featuring the contributor as the murder victim.

The story raised several hundred dollars for the Council, and Mark earned the goodwill of the Council, the readers of the short stories ... and even of the people he killed off. (A few of the contributors became characters in the novel that Mark spun off from those short stories.)

It also exposes a group of potential readers to your work whom you might not otherwise reach with your marketing activities. To maximize this benefit, request that you have the opportunity to read the story or an excerpt at a fundraising event and create an inexpensive chapbook that includes the custom story as well as some of your other works to hand out at the event. Be sure to include links to your purchasable work.

As you can imagine, this can be a time-consuming endeavor. You have to interview the contributor and create a story that has some identifiable connection with them, such as their greatest fear, while also avoiding anything that might be upsetting or triggering for them. You also have to ensure that you have the appropriate legal signoffs from the people whose names are used in the story, both for the story itself and for any expanded use to which you might want to put this material. (Even if you do get their signoff, it's a good idea to include a disclaimer on the copyright page that the characters and places are either fictitious or are used fictitiously. Here's an example of Mark's disclaimer:

The characters and events portrayed in this book are fictitious or are used in a fictious manner. Any similarity to real persons, living or dead, is merely coincidental and not intended by the author.

Due to the complexity and time-consuming nature of custom stories, think carefully before making a commitment to deliver this type of short fiction.

LOCATION-BASED APPS

Location-based apps are a fairly new way of capitalizing on short fiction. The landscape of mobile apps changes rapidly, so it's worthwhile doing a quick search to find out what the offerings are at the time of your investigation, but we have described a few options current as of the publication of this book: **Squirl**, which enables users to discover books set near a location; **Swarm** by FourSquare, which enables users to check in on activities near their location; and **Voicemap**, which enables users to access immersive, GPS-powered audio tours created by local storytellers.

Squirl

The Squirl app (https://squirl.co/) is an attractive option because it's specific to books. You can post a quote from your story and provide buy links to popular retail platforms.

Mark has used Squirl for excerpts from *A Canadian Werewolf in New York* and the short story "This Time Around" flagging key locations in New York: Battery Park (where the protagonist Michael wakes up naked), the Algonquin Hotel (where Michael lives), and the Ed Sullivan Theater (where Michael is scheduled to appear on a talk show). When Squirl users check in near any of those locations, they receive a notification that Mark's story takes place near that location, and when they click the red basket icon, they are given options for purchasing the book:

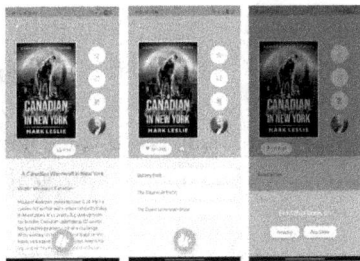

Swarm by FourSquare

As an additional location-based discoverability tool, Mark used FourSquare to create short posts that include excerpts from his works—for example, his non-fiction book *Haunted Hamilton*. The posts are tied to the haunted locations in Hamilton, Ontario, that are discussed in Mark's book. Users of FourSquare's Swarm app (https://swarmapp.com/) see those excerpts as "tips" that pop up as notifications when they check in at different locations. This can be a fun way to increase discoverability, especially if a short story's setting is especially compelling.

VoiceMap

Using VoiceMap.me, a location-based walking tour application, Mark capitalized on the research he had done for *Haunted Hamilton* to build a virtual audio walking tour. App users are prompted to start at a specific location (in this case, the downtown Hamilton Armouries) and the audio, which is triggered when the listener gets to a particular location, shares historic and ghostly tales, then guides them on to the next stop on the tour.

Authors work collaboratively with a VoiceMap editor who guides them through the process of establishing a compelling and easy-to-follow narrative and then getting that narrative recorded. Authors earn 50% of the list price they and VoiceMap set for the tour (generally between $1.99 to $5.99).

You can see Mark's tour at www.voicemap.me/tour/hamilton-ontario or search *hamilton ontario historical downtown ghost walk.*

Mark plans to adapt the short story "This Time Around" into a VoiceMap fictional experience, interlaying the professionally narrated short story which runs 55 minutes with author notes that include details behind the story into an extended walking tour through Manhattan.

There is now a fee for authors to use VoiceMap, so, along with time investment considerations, authors need to consider whether it is a good idea to invest money in this platform.

Resources

Squirl – https://squirl.co/
    FourSquare's Swarm – https://swarmapp.com/
    Voicemap – https://voicemap.me/

WHEN THE READER IS AN AGENT

There is one type of reader with whom a connection can be especially valuable, and that is an agent.

The economics of short fiction writing means that no agent is going to be tempted to represent a short story in the publishing market. Acting as an agent for a piece of short fiction that sells for $300 would earn the agent $30—not much incentive for them to try to deal with a part of the publishing world with which they generally have little experience. But if you are pitching a novel to an agent, having some short fiction on your résumé will illustrate your commitment to your craft and your ability to complete a writing project. And it may not even need to be award-winning or even positively reviewed work. As Lawrence Block writes in *The Liar's Companion: A Field Guide for Fiction Writers*:

The late mystery editor Lee Wright told a friend of mine years ago that anything you happen to publish in a magazine can't hurt you, but that it might help you. In other words, if someone in the business reads a magazine piece of yours ... and thinks it's lousy, he won't hold it against you. ... But if he reads something and loves it, it's to your credit.

As a writer, this kind of connection with a reader who remembers and loves your work is critical. When that reader is someone who is in the business of representing authors in the traditional publishing market, that kind of connection is especially powerful. It is not only a positive reflection on you and your work, but also a demonstration that you have worked professionally, within guidelines, to a deadline, to produce a work that someone else has purchased. It is another feather in your professional cap for the agent to consider when they are deciding whether to represent you and your work.

AS A GIFT

As long as we're thinking of outside-the-box uses for your short fiction, here's an option that is sure to leave an impression, although with a minuscule audience, and one with whom you likely already have a strong connection: using a piece of short fiction as a gift.

Mark wrote a short story for his young goddaughter, Maddie, based on her stuffed horse named Cow—he even had it illustrated by an artist friend. Another friend of Mark, the manager of a bookstore in Ottawa, wrote a Christmas-themed horror short story that took place on Christmas Eve in a bookstore in Ottawa, which he gave to his family members for Christmas. A gift doesn't get much more personal than that—and depending on what the fictional fates of the bookstore manager's family members were, it's a gift that could generate lots of discussion around the Christmas dinner table!

Consider other events that might lend themselves to an appropriately themed short story: a marriage, an anniversary, a graduation. Think of something that will be specifically meaningful to that person: a skydiving story for someone who has always wanted to go skydiving. (Just don't ruin their dream by making something terrible happen in the story!)

Use your talent as a writer to create a special gift for someone.

PART 4
BEST PRACTICES

INTRODUCTION - BEST PRACTICES

This **Best Practices** section covers strategies that apply across the income creation and reader connection goals. The more control you take over the various aspects of getting your short fiction in front of readers—the more roles you play in that process—the more of the chapters in this section will apply to you and your work.

If you are submitting your short fiction to traditional publishing markets, then you will benefit primarily from the "Behind the Curtain: Insights from the Curator's Desk," "Editing and Proofreading," and "Being an Active Member of the Community" chapters. If you are planning to publish a collection of your short stories to the online retail platforms, then all the chapters in this section will apply to your efforts.

We've put this section at the end because we believe it will make more sense after having read the details of the opportunities related to creating income and connecting with readers, but it's a vital companion piece to those earlier sections.

In this section on **Best Practices**, we will cover:

- **Behind the Curtain: Insights from the Curator's Desk** – Gaining perspective on how editors, anthology curators, and contest judges make their choices, and how you can position your work to make the best impression
- **Rights Licensing** – Understanding the implications of granting different rights to third-party publishers
- **Editing and Proofreading** – Managing these processes to ensure professional quality for short fiction
- **Cover Design** – Creating professional, eye-catching covers that reflect your short fiction's genre and tone
- **Links and QR Codes** – Using linking tools to increase income potential and connect readers across your catalog
- **Being an Active Member of the Community** – Building your author platform through active participation in writing and publishing communities

BEHIND THE CURTAIN: INSIGHTS FROM THE CURATOR'S DESK

Behind every contest, magazine, or anthology is a judge, editor or curator, and getting a glimpse of what goes through their minds—and what makes certain pieces rise to the top—can give you a significant advantage when you send your own work out into the world.

Matty and Mark have both served as judges for short fiction contests, and Mark has also served in an editorial position for magazines publishing short fiction and has curated short fiction anthologies. In these roles, we're responsible for sorting through an embarrassment of riches in terms of submissions to select the small percentage that will meet our needs—the most deserving for award recognition, the most well-qualified for publication in a magazine, the most appropriate for inclusion in an anthology. We have had the pleasure of reading hundreds of excellent pieces of short fiction, but excellence in craft is not sufficient for placement.

A magazine might have room to publish only a few of the hundreds of stories they receive each month. An anthology might accommodate only a dozen of thousands of submissions. Curators are looking for stories that comply with their requirements and that hook them in the first sentences and keep them hooked until the very end. They are looking for stories that are so remarkable that they want to tell others about them.

How can you ensure your story is the one that attracts their attention (in a positive way)?

Assess your offering. Some of the entries Matty read for the short fiction contest for which she served as a judge felt more like synopses than meaningful stories on their own. If your story takes 5,000 words to tell, don't shoehorn it into 1,500 to meet the parameters of a particular contest. Similarly, don't allow a contest deadline to rush your work; you want your work to be a gem, not a diamond in the rough. Better to wait for another opportunity than to submit unpolished work.

Once your story is as good as you can make it, ask someone who is a fan of the type of piece you've written to read it before you submit. They might pick up issues like the one that knocked a submission out of the running for Matty: describing a character as "dashing quickly." (When have you seen someone dash slowly?)

Understand the market and the readers. Take time to study the platform you're submitting to and the audience it serves. If possible, read winning entries from previous contests or stories included in earlier volumes of the anthology. Pay attention to the tone—are the stories light and humorous, or dark and unsettling? Are they hopeful, gritty, ironic? Notice the style—does the platform tend to favor traditional narrative structures, or does it lean toward more experimental or avant-garde work? The sponsor of the short fiction contest for which Matty has served as a judge is a mainstream publication with a diverse readership, but several of the entries were so violent or sexually graphic that she couldn't imagine them ever appearing on its pages. Those stories would have done better in an edgier publication or in a contest focused on horror or noir.

Gather any information you can about the demographics of the readership or infer it from the material that has been accepted in the past. This preparation not only increases your chances of acceptance but also ensures that your story will resonate with the readers most likely to appreciate it.

Respect the guidelines. Editors usually publish guidelines for the anthology: required themes or genres they are looking for (and not looking for), whether or not they accept reprints, and the minimum and maximum word count. Editors aren't being arbitrary when they set those guidelines, and this is vital information for potential submitters. Read the guidelines closely. Then re-read them. And comply with them. Some editors will include a unique requirement such as, "We accept standard manuscript format, but please use a font size of 14 instead of 12." They might do this to accommodate a personal preference, but they might also do it to see if the writer is actually paying attention to the guidelines.

It's shocking how many submissions do not comply with even the most basic guidelines. Mark has had writers send him reprints when his guidelines specified only original and unpublished stories. He's had writers send slice-of-life literary ramblings when he was looking for dark tales where superstitions were a central element of the tale. He's had writers submit non-fiction essays to a market that was clearly for fiction and poetry.

Maybe the submitter didn't bother to read the guidelines. Maybe they read them but chose not to comply with them, believing that the brilliance of their work made compliance unnecessary. Maybe they submitted an obviously unsuitable piece of work in the hope that the editor / curator might use it for a different project or pass it along to another editor for whose work it might be appropriate.

Any of these indicate a disrespect for the curator's time.

Disregarding guidelines marks a writer as unprofessional, either as someone who doesn't care enough to do the due diligence expected of someone submitting to a publication or as a creative prima donna who will be difficult to work with. In either case, they've earned a quick rejection.

Read and respect the rules. Some instances of lack of compliance with things like theme or tone can be chalked up to a misinterpretation of guidelines, but rules are unambiguous. If the contest specifies that entries must be 1,500 words or fewer, don't try to sneak in 1,600; look for another contest that accepts longer stories. If the rules specify the margins must be one inch and the font Times New Roman, don't assume that the magnificence of your work will make two-inch margins and Comic Sans acceptable.

These types of rules aren't just editorial quirks—a magazine editor might only have room to accommodate a 1,500-word story, or the production process might depend on consistent formatting across stories.

Make it clean. The vast majority of typos Matty encountered in the submissions she assessed were ones that any writing software's spelling and grammar checker would have caught. Don't ignore those red underlines.

Remember, judges are not looking for excuses to include a work; they're looking for reasons to eliminate it. Lack of compliance with the contest's guidelines? Out. Typos that indicate that the submission was a first draft? Out. There are a lot of excellent short fiction writers out there, and even a seemingly minor slip-up, especially in short-form work, can be fatal.

Following these guidelines won't guarantee you a winning entry, but it will guarantee that you'll give your story the best chance of being considered for those final coveted slots.

And even if you don't land an acceptance on your first approach, you're building a positive relationship with the curator, one that can pay off in the long term. For example, Mark has edited several invite-only anthologies, meaning that rather than accepting open submissions, he reached out to potential contributors. And who did he reach out to? Those short fiction writers he knew from experience would provide the material he needed in a manner that complied with the guidelines and rules he put in place—the true short fiction professionals.

RIGHTS LICENSING

You've gotten an offer to have your short fiction included in a third-party publication? Congratulations! Before you sign, it's important to understand what you're agreeing to—especially when it comes to the rights you're granting.

Of all the sections in this book, this might be the most vital, especially in terms of your ability to earn income from your short fiction. In the first edition of *Taking the Short Tack*, we included information on rights in the "Traditional Publishing" chapter, but in this second edition, we break it out in this Best Practices section, since it can apply across any publishing options—for example, for a writers' group publishing an anthology.

Publishing rights can be broken down along several dimensions:

Media: In what formats will the work be published—print, e-book, audio, or all three? Are they publishing in a magazine, anthology, or standalone edition?

Language: Will the story appear in English only, or is the publisher asking for rights to translate and distribute it in other languages?

Territory: Is the story being licensed for a specific region (e.g., North America, UK) or for worldwide distribution?

Occurrence: Are you selling *first rights* (the first time the story has been published anywhere) or *reprint/second rights* (the story has already been published)?

Term: How long will the publisher hold the rights? Will the rights revert to you automatically after a set period (e.g., six or twelve months), or are you required to request reversion?

Define the rights you're licensing as clearly and narrowly as possible. The more specific the grant of rights, the more flexibility you retain to use the same story again in other formats, languages, or markets—helping that one piece of short fiction continue to work for you long after its initial publication.

As a great example of the benefits of retaining rights to your short fiction, consider this example from Mark:

In 1999, Mark sold first rights for "Browsers," a short story about a bookstore that is to book nerds what a Venus fly trap is to insects, to the magazine *Challenging Destiny*. Mark received semi-pro rate compensation and two contributor's copies of the magazine.

In 2004, Mark reprinted "Browsers" in his short story collection *One Hand Screaming* and printed the story as a standalone chapbook for free distribution at a number of book festivals and author events as a way to promote his writing and to connect with readers.

In 2008, he sold reprint rights for "Browsers" to the anthology *Bound for Evil*, receiving semi-pro rates and two faux-leather hardcover copies of the anthology.

Also in 2008, Mark reprinted "Browsers" in *Active Reader: And Other Cautionary Tales from the Book World*, a print-on-demand chapbook.

In 2015, he released an e-book version of *Active Reader*, which included "Browsers."

In 2017, Mark used Findaway Voices to release the audiobook version of *Active Reader*, including "Browsers."

In 2019, he re-edited and re-released the chapbook in e-book format and print, capitalizing on additional income creation opportunities.

In 2024, he included "Browsers" in the 20th Anniversary edition of *One Hand Screaming* in paperback, hardcover, e-book, and audio.

Mark continues to keep his eyes open for other markets that might be interested in having "Browsers" as a reprint.

This may be an extreme example, but we share it here to give you a sense of what is possible with just one piece of content. Mark's use of "Browsers" across multiple formats, editions, and collections is a strong argument against granting exclusive rights indefinitely. Short fiction thrives on reuse: collections, anthologies, translations, audio editions, bonus content, and more. Keeping your rights diversified gives you the freedom to maximize the story's potential over time.

Resources

The Alliance of Independent Authors' "The Seven Processes of Publishing: Selective Rights Licensing" (https://selfpublishingadvice.org/selective-rights-licensing-for-indie-authors/)

The Indy Author Podcast Episode 107 - The Seventh Process of Publishing: Selective Rights Licensing with Orna Ross (https://www.theindyauthor.com/show-notes/107-orna-ross)

Kristine Kathryn Rusch's blog, "Business Rusch" (www.kriswrites.com/category/business/)

Dean Wesley Smith, *The Magic Bakery: Copyright in the Modern World of Fiction Publishing*, WMG Publishing, 2017.

EDITING AND PROOFREADING

If you're going to ask a reader to take a voyage with you via your short fiction, you owe it to them to send them on that voyage in a seaworthy and leak-proof vessel, and that means editing and proofreading your work to a professional standard.

It's impossible for an author to have enough emotional and intellectual distance from his or her own work to be able to edit it effectively. That's why it's vital to have another person's eyes on your work before you share it with your readers—that's just one of many reasons that we prefer the term *independent publishing* to *self-publishing*. If you approach the publishing endeavor as something you are going to accomplish completely by your*self*, you will miss opportunities to bring your work to a higher standard of excellence.

That said, there are steps you yourself can take to ensure that when you share your piece of short fiction with others for editing and proofreading, it will be as clean as possible.

Read Your Work Aloud

We highly recommend investing the time to read your work aloud before you send it to your editor.

- Reading aloud forces a slower pace that enables you to catch content mistakes you might otherwise miss (to use an example from one of Matty's pre-editor self-edits, catching a reference to "twenty-first century office buildings" in a flashback that takes place in 1999).
- It's easier to catch awkward repetition of a word or other authorial tics by hearing the material than by reading it silently. (Matty's Achilles' heel? Having her characters sigh too much. For Mark? Because his werewolf character Michael Andrews relies on his sense of smell, many of his pages are infused with the stench of numerous olfactory mentions.)
- Absorbing the content in a way that is different from the normal visual mode can highlight where you need to adjust for clarity—for example, judicious addition of commas to signal pauses, or a few extra *he said*s and *she said*s in long stretches of dialogue.
- You can use the read-through as an opportunity to capture and write out phonetically any tricky words for the audiobook narration.
- You can get a sense of whether you might be a candidate for recording your own audiobook.
- If you record some of the passages that you think you might want to use for readings, you can use the recording to become extra-familiar with them.

After incorporating the changes from your own read-through, consider taking the additional step of listening to the text using a built-in text-to-speech feature. Most modern devices include accessibility settings that can read text aloud. Alternatively, browser-based tools like Natural Reader offer free, natural-sounding narration and don't require a separate app download.

Anything that enables you to bring fresh eyes—and ears—to words that you have already read dozens if not hundreds of times can help you identify editorial issues. This might be something as simple as using a print-out rather than reading on the screen or changing the font or text color.

Enlisting the Help of Others

If you want to capitalize on the *short* of short fiction to benefit from the opportunities for a faster publication schedule than is possible for novel-length works, then you lose one method writers can use to gain some editorial distance from their work: putting it aside for a week or a month in order to be able to return to it after that time with fresh eyes.

But *short* also opens up options for making the editorial process manageable logistically and financially that would be more difficult to pursue for longer works.

For one, the length of the work means that getting it edited will be far less costly than getting a novel edited.

If you can find an editor who writes and publishes short fiction themselves, you'll get the added benefit that they can provide not only structural, stylistic, and grammatical input, but may also be able to advise you on the markets for which your work might be a good fit.

You can find inexpensive proofreading services through writers' groups. Matty has offered advance reader copies of her works to fellow writers' group members with an offer of a "typo bounty"—$5 per typo to some maximum amount.

Mark has sold stories to charity markets and, in lieu of payment, received a professional edit on the story. After the terms of the initial release are complete, he has sold that work to another market as a reprint or published it on his own.

The shortness of the work also opens some alternatives to a pay-for-service editor. For example, you might ask members of your writing or critique group to provide input on your stories, and the fact that the work is short means that you're requesting a relatively small time commitment. This approach works best if the reader not only has some demonstrated editorial skills but also enjoys the type of short fiction you are writing.

Remember the importance of being a good citizen of the writing and publishing communities: if you request editorial assistance from writer friends and colleagues, make sure you are prepared to return the favor.

Resources

Natural Readers – Free text-to-speech service (www.natural readers.com/online/)

COVER DESIGN

Just as there are low-cost options to accommodate the editing and proofreading requirements of professional-level short fiction, there are ways of reducing the cost of an attractive cover design.

Pro + DIY

Since it's the rare individual who is equally talented in writing and in visual design, we generally discourage authors from designing their own covers, but you can capitalize on pro design while benefiting from the cost savings of do it yourself. For example, Matty has a design professional create the covers of the Ann Kinnear Suspense Novels and is then able to use that design as a template for covers for her Suspense Shorts, creating the shorts' covers using Canva and purchased stock images. Below is an example of the cover of one of the novels, *The Sense of Death*, and of one of Matty's short stories, *All Deaths Endure*. (Matty made the text on the short story cover bolder since, unlike the novels, which are available in print, the shorts are only available as e-books and the covers are seen only in small thumbnails on the retail sites.)

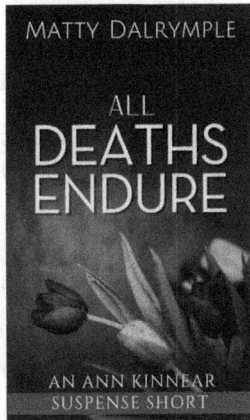

The key to the success of such covers is that they:

•Are simple—no complex Photoshop work going on here

•Conform to the overall look of the covers of the Ann Kinnear Suspense Novels

•Use a small number of visually compatible fonts – Often design tools will offer font families (e.g., Alegreya SC, Alegreya Sans Black, Alegreya Sans Thin, etc.) and sticking with one or two fonts within that family will ensure that they are visually pleasing together.

Matty purchases the images she uses from stock image sites that provide clear licenses for commercial use. While free image resources are available, we recommend investing in paid images. Doing so ensures that you have a solid license for your work, reduces the risk of seeing the same "free" image on countless other covers or ads, and supports the artists who create these visuals. The cost is usually modest, but the professional polish and originality it adds to your short fiction projects can make a meaningful difference.

As with any book cover, compare any design against the covers of other successful stories in your genre to ensure that it will appeal to the readers you want to reach.

Pre-designed Covers

Another budget-friendly option for short fiction is to use a pre-designed book cover. Many professional cover designers offer pre-made templates: high-quality designs that are sold only once, with placeholder text that is customized with your title, author name, and subtitle. These covers often cost a fraction of what custom covers do, sometimes as little as $25–$75 USD, and they can deliver a polished, genre-appropriate look without the higher price tag or turnaround time of a bespoke design.

Pre-designed covers are especially useful for standalone short stories, where the financial return may not justify a major investment in design. They are also a good option for authors producing a high volume of short fiction or experimenting with multiple genres or styles. The key is to look for a design that fits your genre, tone, and author brand, and—just like with DIY designs—to compare it to current bestsellers in your category.

(A potential downside of using pre-designed covers for

multiple related short stories—for example, Matty's Ann Kinnear Suspense Shorts—is that you can't be sure that you will be able to find visually consistent covers across all the stories.)

There are numerous pre-designed cover options available— you can find providers vetted by the Alliance of Independent Authors' Watchdog Desk at https://selfpublishingadvice.org/ best-self-publishing-services/. Check out BookCovers.com (https://bookcovers.com/, formerly SelfPubBookCovers.com), which is owned by Draft2Digital.

Resources

Easy-to-use design tool with templates – canva.com, book brush.com

BookCovers.com —— Pre-designed book covers for purchase – https://bookcovers.com/

The Alliance of Independent Authors' Self-Publishing Services ratings (https://selfpublishingadvice.org/best-self-publishing-services/)

LINKS AND QR CODES

Retail Platform Links

Just as providing links (hyperlinks in e-books, text references in print) to your other works is vital to gain the most income creation and reader connection benefit from your work, make sure that on the online retail platforms, your short fiction work is linked to the works to which you want to funnel readers. A reader should be able to search for your author name and find not only your short fiction but also any novels or other works. For Amazon, be sure you claim all your titles via Amazon Author Central; this is the mechanism Amazon uses to display all your offerings on your books' product pages.

On Kobo Writing Life and Draft2Digital, if you enter the same series name (e.g., *The Ann Kinnear Suspense Shorts*) in the work's metadata, the related works will be systematically linked so that a customer who sees one of the works in the series can easily access the other items in the series. On Kindle Direct Publishing, there's an additional *Create Series* option within your author Bookshelf that allows you to connect books by series.

Also ensure that all the formats (print, e-book, audio) of a single work appear on that work's product page on the online retailer. This ensures that promotion for one format will have a halo effect on the visibility to and sales of the other formats. It's not uncommon for a BookBub e-book Featured Deal, for example, to also result in an increase in sales for the print and audio formats of that book. In the best case, a customer might purchase your work in multiple formats. If you don't see all available formats on the product detail page, contact the customer service team for that retailer (e.g., KDP for Amazon).

Books2Read Universal Links

One of the easiest ways to manage links to your works is through a universal book link creator like Books2Read.

Books2Read is a service created by Draft2Digital and is available to all authors, even those not publishing through D2D. You enter a link to your book on one of the retail sites, and an automated crawler will find links to that book on other websites, then create a master URL link that includes all the major retail sites on which your book is available. It also uses geo-targeting to ensure that the customer goes to the correct location of the website. (Amazon, Apple, and Kobo all have different versions of their websites for different global territories that display different default prices.)

When a customer / reader clicks on a Books2Read link, they see the book, plus links to all of the retailers where that book is available (using the most up-to-date authorized version of each retailer's logo).

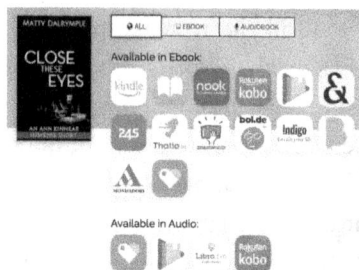

When that reader clicks on a specific retailer icon, it takes them to the e-book's landing page on that retailer. It will also offer a pop-up that asks the reader if they'd like to set that retailer as their default store. If they do, the next time they follow any Books2Read link for any other book, it will automatically take them directly to that store.

Books2Read links can be customized to make their purpose clearer and easier to remember. For example, Matty customized the link to her Ann Kinnear suspense short story *Close These Eyes* to https://books2read.com/Close-These-Eyes.

Using a universal link to all retailers will save you from having to manage dozens of different links for every book, including the links in the back of those books. For example, if you are uploading your e-book to different platforms—Amazon, Apple, Barnes & Noble, etc.—you can use one file containing a universal link rather than creating a separate file for each platform.

Alternatively, if you use Vellum to generate the e-book files needed by the various platforms (highly recommended), and if you provide Vellum with the appropriate metadata, then Vellum will manage the insertion of the appropriate link (an Amazon link for a Kindle reader, a Nook link for a Barnes & Noble reader, and so on).

Books2Read Reading Lists

As well as providing an easy mechanism for creating universal links, Books2Read also enables the creation of reading lists. Below is a list that Matty created for the Ann Kinnear Suspense Shorts at the customized URL www.books2read.com/rl/ann_kinnear_suspense_shorts.

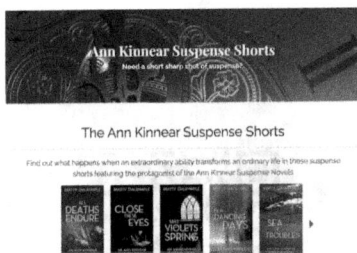

The Ann Kinnear Suspense Shorts

Find out what happens when an extraordinary ability transforms an ordinary life in these suspense shorts featuring the protagonist of the Ann Kinnear Suspense Novels

You can see that Books2Read enables you to create a virtual collection of your works, as Matty has done here.

You can also create a listing of titles from different authors on a theme, as Mark did with his "Boos 2 Read" landing page (www.books2read.com/rl/boos2read/), which features Halloween-themed reads in different genres—novels, short stories, and collections. He also created a landing page called "Spooky Spaces" (www.books2read.com/rl/spookyspaces) spotlighting some of his true ghost story titles alongside similar books by other authors.

The Books2Read reading lists not only provide an elegant way of presenting groupings of books to your readers to boost discoverability of all your short fiction—thereby increasing their income generation potential—but also can generate additional income if you use retailer affiliate links such as those available through the Amazon Associates program.

QR Codes

We all became familiar with QR codes during the pandemic, when many restaurants replaced physical menus with scannable QR codes accessing online information. People are less perplexed by these codes than they might have been pre-pandemic, and QR codes provide an easy way to direct readers to online resources. The codes can even be branded, as with this example of a QR code that Mark used on a giveaway postcard that he handed out at a horror fan conference:

QR Tiger is one commonly used service for create QR codes; Canva also offers apps for QR code creation.

Shortened URLs

You can shorten URLs to make their destination clearer and to make them easier to say—for example, if you want to reference a particular site in an interview. Bitly.com and TinyURL.com are two popular tools for shortening and customizing URLs. Note that Bitly's free plan may insert an interstitial page that shows a preview of the destination and includes ads. See the Resources section for some options for creating QR codes.

Resources

Books2Read Universal link creator – Enables the reader to go to one landing page that will provide links to all the major online retailers (www.books2read.com/)

Books2Read Reading Lists – Free service to create a web page that groups together multiple books (yours and/or other authors'). To access the Reading Lists creation and editing tools, log onto your Books2Read account and, from the LINK TOOLS tab in the header, click the Reading Lists option.)

QR Tiger –https://www.qrcode-tiger.com/

Canva – Includes a number of QR code-creation apps

Bitly.com or TinyURL.com – Create shortened, customizable URL links. Note that Bitly's free plan may insert an interstitial page that shows a preview of the destination and includes ads.

Vellum – Mac-based formatting software that lives up to its tagline, "Create Beautiful Books" (easily, we would add). Enables simple generation of pdf files for print and epub files for e-books. (www.vellum.pub/)

BEING AN ACTIVE MEMBER OF THE COMMUNITY

Although not specific to creating income or connecting with readers via short fiction, you can improve your chances of success in using the strategies and tactics described in this book by understanding your role in and responsibility to the larger writing and publishing community.

Mark's first professional short story sale came from a relationship he had established with the editor years earlier. In fact, there are at least a dozen short story publications in the past ten years that Mark derived specifically from relationships he nurtured with other writers and editors that he worked with within the writing, publishing, and bookselling communities.

Before Matty was invited to contribute a story to a writers' group anthology, she had presented a pro bono overview of author self-promotion for that group. She opened the opportunity for a coauthored reader magnet by being an active participant in a genre writers' organization.

This is not to imply that every transaction in the writing and publishing worlds is a quid pro quo; you'll do plenty of favors for other authors that they may never have a chance to return and will receive favors from other authors that you may not have a chance to reciprocate. Instead, we posit that you will have a smoother writing and publishing journey if you are actively involved in those communities and look for opportunities to pay it forward to your fellow authors.

This book is filled with strategies and tactics that are even more likely to be successful if you engage in this kind of active involvement. Would you like to participate in an anthology? Don't just sit back and wait for the invitations to come in— discuss the possibility of creating an anthology at a writers' group meeting. Wondering about the ins and outs of a foreign rights deal? Find a book on that topic and then be so bold as to drop the author a note thanking them for the resource and perhaps seeking clarification on a detail. Want to optimize your technical set-up so that you can start posting audios or videos of your short fiction to social media? Query your friends for subject matter experts and then, if they want to expand their services to other authors, talk them up within the community of people who may have the same need.

This book wouldn't have come about if Mark hadn't spun up the *Stark Reflections on Writing and Publishing* podcast with a goal of helping fellow authors with this free resource, if Matty (as a loyal listener of the podcast) hadn't requested an episode specific to opportunities for short fiction, if Mark hadn't obliged, and if Matty hadn't proposed this co-authored project.

Success in the writing and publishing worlds is not a zero-sum game. It is, to use one of Matty's favorite nautical metaphors, a case of a rising tide raising all boats.

AFTERWORD

There's always more to explore when it comes to short fiction. Whether you're new to the form or have a drawer full of stories waiting to find their audience, each piece offers fresh potential for income and connection.

Short fiction lets us test new ideas, revisit favorite characters, build bridges to new readers, and offer loyal fans something extra. It's a form that reflects our rapidly evolving publishing landscape: versatile, responsive, and rich with possibility.

We hope the guidance in *Taking the Short Tack* helps you make the most of those possibilities. Whatever your creative and business goals are, your stories deserve to be read, shared, and celebrated. Keep navigating the currents, keep adjusting your course, and keep writing.

And when your short fiction finds a new way to reach readers, we'd love to hear about it.

Matty@MattyDalrymple.com

Mark@MarkLeslie.ca

PART 5

RESOURCES SUMMARY

RESOURCES SUMMARY

For easy reference, we have consolidated the Resources referenced in each chapter in this summary.

Traditional Publishing Market

Douglas Smith's *Playing the Short Game: How to Market and Sell Short Fiction* (2nd *Edition*)

The Indy Author Podcast Episode 193 - The Path to Short Story Publication with Michael Bracken

Submission Search Engines / Tools / Trackers

- Duotrope (duotrope.com) and Submittable (submittable.com) – Enable searches for appropriate markets; used by a number of traditional publishing platforms as their submission tool

Other Publication Listings

- *The Write Life* article "Where to Submit Short Stories: 23 Magazines and Websites That Want

Your Work" (www.thewritelife.com/where-to-submit-short-stories/)

Submission Guidelines

- Proper Manuscript Format – Each market has its own submission guidelines (and violating them is a quick way into the reject pile) but William Shun's *Proper Manuscript Format* (www.shunn.net/format/story.html)is a reference cited by many markets. Note that one update to this venerable document is that submission in Courier font is no longer recommended. You'll find other guidance related to manuscript format at the following:
- https://reedsy.com/studio/resources/book-manuscript-format
- https://www.writersdigest.com/getting-published/follow-industry-typing-and-formatting-conventions-for-your-writing-genre
- https://www.sfwa.org/2005/01/04/manuscript-format/

Standalone e-books

James Scott Bell's *How to Write Short Stories And Use Them to Further Your Writing Career* – Offers tips on set-up of short fiction on Amazon's KDP platform

Audio

Voice by INaudio (formerly Findaway Voices) (https://www.inaudio.com/)

Author's Republic – From Author's Republic's website:

"Author's Republic is more than just an audiobook publisher. We're a new solution for getting your audiobook onto more platforms and in front of more listeners in the easiest way ever." (www.authorsrepublic.com/)

Chirp – BookBub's audiobook promotion platform (https://www.chirpbooks.com/home)

Patron Support

Patreon – A membership platform that enables supporters to provide financial support to creators (www.patreon.com/)

Buy Me a Coffee (www.buymeacoffee.com/) and tiny-Coffee (www.wpplugindirectory.org/tinycoffee/) – Enable supporters to provide financial support to creators

Foreign Language Markets

Douglas Smith Article: Selling to Foreign Markets (www.smithwriter.com/FML_article)

Douglas Smith's Foreign Market List (www.smithwriter.com/foreign_market_list.htm)

Kristine Kathryn Rusch, "Subsidiary Rights for Indies" (https://kriswrites.com/2017/10/11/business-musings-subsidiary-rights-for-indies/)

ScribeShadow – AI-powered translation (https://www.scribeshadow.com/)

Getting Unstuck

The Indy Author Podcast:

Episode 164 - What Writers Can Learn from Short Fiction with Gabriela Pereira

Episode 192 - Stretching Your Writing Muscles with Short Fiction with Richie Narvaez

Offering Your Story for Free

BookFunnel (www.bookfunnel.com/)
StoryOrigin (https://storyoriginapp.com/)

Author Readings

For an in-depth discussion of the best practices for author readings, check out the book Matty coauthored with M.L. Ronn, *From Page to Platform: How to Succeed as an Author Speaker.*

Flash Fiction and Micro-Fiction

Stark Reflections on Writing and Publishing Episode 366 – Bolts of Fiction with Daniel Willcocks and Sam Frost - https://starkreflections.ca/2024/06/15/episode-366-bolts-of-fiction-with-daniel-willcocks-and-sam-frost/

The Indy Author Podcast Episode 098 - Redefining Indy Success through Short Fiction with Ran Walker

Generally the resources we mention are focused on the business of short fiction, but we can't resist including a recommendation for Ran Walker's charming *One Hundred Ways: A Handbook for Writing 100-Word Stories*, which, appropriately enough, is comprised of one hundred hundred-word chapters.

Location-based Apps

Squirl – https://squirl.co/
FourSquare's Swarm – https://swarmapp.com/
Voicemap – https://voicemap.me/

Rights Licensing

The Alliance of Independent Authors' "The Seven Processes of Publishing: Selective Rights Licensing" (https://selfpublishin gadvice.org/selective-rights-licensing-for-indie-authors/)

The Indy Author Podcast Episode 107 - The Seventh Process of Publishing: Selective Rights Licensing with Orna Ross (https://www.theindyauthor.com/show-notes/107-orna-ross)

Kristine Kathryn Rusch's blog, "Business Rusch" (www.kriswrites.com/category/business/)

Dean Wesley Smith, *The Magic Bakery: Copyright in the Modern World of Fiction Publishing*, WMG Publishing, 2017.

Editing and Proofreading

Natural Readers – Free text-to-speech service (www.natural readers.com/online/)

Cover Design

Easy-to-use design tool with templates – canva.com, book brush.com

BookCovers.com — Pre-designed book covers for purchase – https://bookcovers.com/

The Alliance of Independent Authors' Self-Publishing Services ratings (https://selfpublishingadvice.org/best-self-publishing-services/)

Links and QR Codes

Books2Read Universal link creator – Enables the reader to go to one landing page that will provide links to all the major online retailers (www.books2read.com/)

Books2Read Reading Lists – Free service to create a web page that groups together multiple books (yours and/or other authors'). To access the Reading Lists creation and editing tools, log onto your Books2Read account and, from the LINK TOOLS tab in the header, click the Reading Lists option.)

QR Tiger –https://www.qrcode-tiger.com/

Canva – Includes a number of QR code-creation apps

Bitly.com or TinyURL.com – Create shortened, customizable URL links. Note that Bitly's free plan may insert an interstitial page that shows a preview of the destination and includes ads.

Vellum – Mac-based formatting software that lives up to its tagline, "Create Beautiful Books" (easily, we would add). Enables simple generation of pdf files for print and epub files for e-books. (www.vellum.pub/)

IF YOU HAVE any questions or comments about this book, or have other resources you'd like to let us know about, please e-mail us:

matty@mattydalrymple.com

mark@markleslie.ca

Thank you for joining us on this journey!

ALSO BY MATTY DALRYMPLE

The Lizzy Ballard Thrillers

Rock Paper Scissors (Book 1)

Snakes and Ladders (Book 2)

The Iron Ring (Book 3)

Kill Box Checkmate (Book 3½)

Scare Card (Book 4)

Drawing Dead (Book 5)

The Lizzy Ballard Thrillers Ebook Box Set

The Ann Kinnear Suspense Novels

The Sense of Death (Book 1)

The Sense of Reckoning (Book 2)

The Falcon and the Owl (Book 3)

A Furnace for Your Foe (Book 4)

A Serpent's Tooth (Book 5)

Be with the Dead (Book 6)

The Ann Kinnear Suspense Novels Ebook Box Set - Books 1-3

The Ann Kinnear Suspense Shorts

All Deaths Endure

Close These Eyes

May Violets Spring

Ministers of Grace

Our Dancing Days

Sea of Troubles

Stage of Fools

Write in Water

Non-Fiction

Taking the Short Tack: Creating Income and Connecting with Readers Using Short Fiction with Mark Leslie Lefebvre

The Indy Author's Guide to Podcasting for Authors: Creating Connections, Community, and Income

From Page to Platform: How to Succeed as an Author Speaker with M.L. Ronn

Collaborate to Create: A Guide to Coauthoring Nonfiction with M.L. Ronn

The Podcast Guest Playbook: Turning Conversations into Connections and Community with Mark Leslie Lefebvre

ALSO BY MARK LESLIE LEFEBVRE

Non-fiction: Writing and Publishing

The 7 Ps of Publishing Success

Killing It on Kobo

An Author's Guide to Working with Libraries and Bookstores

Wide for the Win

Publishing Pitfalls for Authors

Accounting for Authors (with D.F. Hart)

The Podcast Guest Playbook (with Matty Dalrymple)

The Relaxed Author (with Joanna Penn)

Canadian Werewolf

This Time Around

A Canadian Werewolf in New York

Stowe Away

Fear and Longing in Los Angeles

Fright Nights, Big City

Lover's Moon (with Julie Strauss)

Hex and the City (with Julie Strauss)

Only Monsters in the Building

The Desmond Files

Evasion

Sin Eater

Collateral Damage

I, Death

Short Story Collections

One Hand Screaming: 20 Haunting Years

Active Reader: And Other Cautionary Tales from the Book World

Bumps in the Night: Creepy Campfire Tales

Snowman Shivers

Halloween Treats

Nocturnal Screams: Night Cries

Nocturnal Screams: Ode to Classics

Nocturnal Screams: Dark Shadows

Nocturnal Screams: Literary Haunts

Nocturnal Screams: Unexpected Strangers

Nocturnal Screams: Something Wicked

Nocturnal Screams: Z is for Zombie

Nocturnal Screams: Phantom Itch

Short Stories

A Murder of Scarecrows

Spirits

Collateral Damage

Anthologies (as editor)

Campus Chills

Tesseracts Sixteen: Parnassus Unbound

Fiction River: Editor's Choice

Fiction River: Feel the Fear

Fiction River: Superstitious

Obsessions

Halloween Harvest

Pulphouse Fiction Magazine

Non-fiction: Paranormal / Ghost Stories

Haunted Hamilton

Spooky Sudbury

Tomes of Terror

Creepy Capital

Haunted Hospitals

Macabre Montreal

ABOUT THE AUTHOR

Matty Dalrymple is the author of the Lizzy Ballard Thrillers, beginning with *Rock Paper Scissors*; the Ann Kinnear Suspense Novels, beginning with *The Sense of Death*; and the Ann Kinnear Suspense Shorts, including *Close These Eyes*. She is a member of International Thriller Writers and Sisters in Crime. Go to https://www.mattydalrymple.com/ > About to learn more and to sign up for her occasional email newsletter.

Matty also educates and advocates for writers as The Indy Author. She is the host and producer of hundreds of episodes of *The Indy Author Podcast* and has spoken on topics related to writing and publishing at events such as the Writer's Digest annual conference, the Alliance of Independent Authors' Self-PubCon, Author Nation, Authors Guild webinars, International Thriller Writers' CraftFest, and many more. She writes nonfiction books for writers, and her articles have appeared in *Writer's Digest* magazine, *Indie Author Magazine*, and ALLi's *The Indie Author* magazine. She serves as ALLi's Campaigns Manager. Go to www.theindyauthor.com/ > About & Contact for more information about Matty's non-fiction work and to sign up for her weekly email newsletter.

Matty lives with her husband, Wade Walton, and their dogs in Chester County, Pennsylvania, and enjoys vacationing on Mount Desert Island, Maine, and Sedona, Arizona, and these locations provide the settings for her novels.

facebook.com/matty.dalrymple

ABOUT THE AUTHOR

Mark Leslie Lefebvre (le-FAVE) is the author (as Mark Leslie) of numerous horror short stories and curator / editor of horror anthologies. He writes, speaks, consults, and podcasts based on his more than a quarter-century of experience in writing, publishing, and bookselling. He established the Kobo Writing Life author program and is the Director of Business Development at Draft2Digital. Find out more at www.markleslie.ca/.

ISBN-13: 978-1-959882-28-2 – Ebook edition

ISBN-13: 978-1-959882-29-9 – Paperback edition

www.ingramcontent.com/pod-product-compliance
Lightning Source LLC
Chambersburg PA
CBHW072145270326
41931CB00010B/1887